UNDER MY HELMET

UNDER MY HELMET

HELMET

A Football Player's Lifelong

Battle with Bipolar Disorder

KEITH O'NEIL

FOREWORD BY TONY DUNGY

Skyhorse Publishing

Skyhorse Publishing books may be purchased in bulk at special discounts for sales promotion, corporate gifts, fund-raising, or educational purposes. Special editions can also be created to specifications. For details, contact the Special Sales Department, Skyhorse Publishing, 307 West 36th Street, 11th Floor, New York, NY 10018 or info@skyhorsepublishing.com.

Skyhorse® and Skyhorse Publishing® are registered trademarks of Skyhorse Publishing, Inc.®, a Delaware corporation.

Visit our website at www.skyhorsepublishing.com.

10 9 8 7 6 5 4 3 2 1

Library of Congress Cataloging-in-Publication Data is available on file.

Cover design by Tom Lau

Cover image: iStockphoto

Print ISBN: 978-1-5107-1686-5

Ebook ISBN: 978-1-5107-1688-9

Printed in the United States of America

For my beautiful wife Jill and sons Connor and Tanner,

and for all those living with a silent illness

TABLE OF CONTENTS

Author's Note

Under My Helmet is not about concussions or chronic traumatic encephalopathy (CTE). Those subjects are important and potentially tragic. They affect too many who play football, including in the NFL, as well as other athletes and those who participate in high-risk activities.

Under My Helmet is about a condition that affects far more people than that. You don't have to make a single tackle to be affected. Those close to us who are impacted—and we each know many of them, some of whose conditions remain hidden from us—are just regular people. They did not put themselves in harm's way.

It happens that I played football. But this is not really about football.

Foreword by Tony Dungy

I first met Keith O'Neil in September of 2005. I was the head coach of the Indianapolis Colts, and our scouting department told us he was a player who could help our team. Keith was a very good athlete who was tough, aggressive, and had a tremendous work ethic. In short, he was our kind of player. After doing a little research, there was another reason I was drawn to him. Keith's father, Ed O'Neil, had been a player for my favorite team growing up, the Detroit Lions. I had watched Ed play, and I knew if Keith was anything like his dad, he would certainly be an asset to us. We had an opening at linebacker, his position, and we decided Keith would upgrade our football team.

When Keith arrived, he had the look of a young man who had everything you could ask for in life. He was joining a team that had an opportunity to win a Super Bowl. He was going to make a good sum of money playing the game he loved. He had a beautiful fiancée, Jill, and his future seemed so bright. Once Keith got on the field, he picked up our defenses very quickly and fit right in with our group of players. After just one week of practice, we were very confident we'd made a good decision. Keith was going to be an integral part of our team, and he was in our game plan as we were preparing to open up the regular season against the Baltimore Ravens.

As we were making final preparations to fly to Baltimore, Keith told me he needed to see me. I thought he may have wanted some clarification on the schedule or what we were expecting of him, and what his role might be going forward. That is what most new players want to know. But what Keith shared with me in my office caught me completely off guard. He said he was having difficulty adjusting to this new situation. He was having trouble sleeping because he was very anxious and didn't think he could make the trip with us to Baltimore. At first I thought he merely needed some encouragement, that he wasn't sure how well he was performing on the field. I told him he was doing exceptionally well and the coaches were very happy with how he was doing. He would be a big part of our special teams units while he continued to learn the nuances of our defense.

But as we talked a little more, I could see that it wasn't the uncertainty of how he was performing that was bothering Keith. It was what was going on in his life and, more specifically, what was going on in his mind. He was apprehensive about the whole situation. Moving from Dallas to

Indianapolis, learning a new system, making new friends, finding a place to live, hoping his fiancée could adjust to this new life, as well. It was all starting to overwhelm him, and he needed some time to sort it out. He asked me if it would be okay if he didn't travel with the team to Baltimore. He felt he needed to spend some time with Jill and work things out.

That was definitely a first for me. Normally, I was the one telling players that they wouldn't be making the trip, that they needed to keep working hard, and eventually their chance would come. But here was Keith, with the opportunity he had worked for his entire life, telling me he didn't think he was ready to play at the moment. The more we talked, I could see that there were deeper issues. I didn't know what was at the root of his problem, but I knew we had people on our support staff who could help.

We believed in Keith and wanted to help him. I told him not to worry about the Baltimore game that week. We were concerned about the big picture, the entire season and, more importantly, about his emotional health. We decided he would take the weekend and spend it with Jill, but we also wanted him to visit with our medical people and see if we could help him with this anxiety issue.

That was just the start, as Keith still had a great deal of personal anguish to confront.

I am delighted to tell you that this story has a happy ending. While Keith went on to play some outstanding football for us, and his contributions helped us the following year to beat the Chicago Bears in Super Bowl XLI, the more important development was that Keith was eventually diagnosed as having Bipolar disorder. Through the same grit he showed on the field, he was able to get much-needed help from so many caring people. He is now married and has two beautiful children but, more than that, has a feeling of control over his life.

Everyone in the National Football League has the goal of winning a Super Bowl. Keith has done that, and I know he is very proud of that accomplishment. But I believe that writing this book is even more significant than winning a Super Bowl. Since being diagnosed, Keith has made it his mission to help other people who are suffering from mental illnesses. He wants to let people know that there is no shame in having a mental illness—it is no different than a physical ailment. If you see the right doctors and follow the right treatment plan, you can improve, and even be healed.

Keith and I have stayed in touch over the years, and I'm extremely proud of him. I always felt our job as NFL players and coaches was not just to win games, but to make our communities better places to live. I'm just happy that Keith had the courage to come into my office that day and tell me something was wrong. That was the start of his recovery process, and I pray that there may be someone who reads this book and it starts them on their way to healing.

Thank you, Keith, for opening up your heart and your life to help others.

Tony Dungy
May 2017

Introduction

There was a method to my madness.

Sunday, the most important workday for anyone lucky enough to play in the National Football League, I was sprinting down the field with the kickoff unit, leading the charge, with my new teammates from the Indianapolis Colts. I had been picked up the previous month after getting cut by the Dallas Cowboys, where I'd spent two seasons playing special teams and the occasional down at linebacker. Now, I was running hard, #53, in my white and blue-striped Colts road uniform. There's an eerie quiet you experience when wearing a football helmet, the sound of breathing almost like an

astronaut's but faster, the whoosh inside intense and menac-
ing and private—and odd, contrasted with what I was doing
at the moment: racing down field, jacked to make something
explosive happen.

Anyone who plays on special teams, especially at the NFL
level, has to be a little bit nuts. "It isn't normal for two grown
men of that size and strength to want to run into each other
at full speed," says my father, Ed, a former All-America linebacker at Penn State, first-round draft choice of the Detroit
Lions, and longtime football coach. And no play in football
is more full speed than a special teams play: kickoff, kickoff
return, punt, punt return. (Special teams also includes field
goal and extra point tries, but they don't move anywhere near
that speed.) I was one of the few chosen to play on all four.

It's a form of madness. "Acceptable" madness.

It was early October 2005, sunny and warm and clear,
and we were at the Tennessee Titans' home stadium, in Nash-
ville. Seven minutes into the second half, we were up 21–0,
after Peyton Manning's third touchdown pass of the day.
Our placekicker lofted the ball to the Titans' return man,
who was protected behind a "wedge" of four other Titans. I
was the first Colt to reach their 30-yard line because I was
fast: Speed was one of my assets as a football player. If you're
6-foot, 240 pounds (after a big dessert), small by NFL linebacker standards, you'd better have some other things going
for you. For me it was speed, being a very hard hitter, having
good instincts on gaps and changes of direction, and a willingness to do just about anything my coaches asked.

My job, the craziest of the crazy special teams jobs, was to
"bust" the wedge. It's a pretty simple idea: You give up your
body so your teammates can make an easier tackle from the

chaos you create. Normally you go right at the guy who's the point of the wedge and try to take him out and hope that the collision slows down other players of theirs—especially the ballcarrier—because you've limited his lanes. The special teams coach for the Colts had me line up on kickoffs so that I would be the wedge buster. They must have seen film of what I had done on the Cowboys to want me to do the same for them.

At one of my first meetings with the Colts special teams unit, the coach told us about something he called the "Horizontal Mambo": As you approach the wedge, you jump up, fling sideways (horizontal), and use your body to sweep away anyone and everyone you can reach at the point of the spear, the way a bowling pin gets knocked down, swings wide, and knocks down other pins. Only in this case, since you're airborne, you're knocking them over high up, not low down. If you attempted a Horizontal Mambo, you wouldn't expect to take out the ballcarrier, who's a few yards behind the wedge, but you would seriously mess up his protection and rhythm.

"I've been coaching over twenty years and no one's ever done it," the special teams coach teased us. "I'll give a hundred bucks to anyone who does."

No one on the unit, not me or anyone else, tried it the first three games of the season. To be honest, I wasn't thinking about the dare at all. Then, in the middle of the third quarter of our fourth game, as I was running downfield against the Titans, I saw my opening.

When I hit the 30-yard-line, I saw the wedge coming right at me. In the instant just before the collision, I thought: *Do it.*

I jumped up, twisted my body horizontally, while also diving at them, as if the blockers were a body of water I was leaping into. But in my excitement I actually mistimed my jump. I didn't quite take out both front guys. One of them crumpled to the ground, and after the play he would stagger off the field, diagnosed later with a concussion. The player to his left got displaced but kept his feet. Because of the crazy angle of my attack, I hit the lead wedge guy in the crown of his helmet with my tailbone, which would later cause massive bruising and swelling all the way down into my groin.

It was not as devastating to their wedge as I had hoped. But no way did they expect me to do that. No way did anyone expect it, which made it effective. There was method to my madness.

TV announcer Kevin Harlan and former San Francisco 49ers offensive lineman Randy Cross were covering the game for CBS. "You hear the old term, about how an NFL game is like a car accident on your body?" said Cross. (I didn't hear about his comments until after the game, of course.) "Well, there's a one-play, three-car pileup. Having no regard for your body . . . how much do you think [O'Neil] cares about yours if you're in the wedge? How about, absolutely none?"

At the team meeting the next day, Colts head coach Tony Dungy awarded me a game ball. (I also had a forced fumble and made three tackles on special teams.) The following week in San Francisco, against the 49ers, I was named special teams captain and later given what we called the "Charles Bronson Award" for two more badass plays—plays where you're under control but what you make happen looks almost out of control, the kind of bang-bang play that makes the NFL the NFL. The kind of thing that even my father, a football lifer, says "isn't normal." Where you turn order into disorder, because that's the point.

This is the story of a man who tried to keep order until it became evident to himself and everyone else that he could not. Until, eventually, there was no method, only madness.

It's my story.

Chapter 1

THE BEAR

An interesting question about mental illness: Where does the sometimes unpleasant personality end and the illness begin? Would you act much differently if you didn't have something "wrong" with you—or are you by nature ornery (for instance) or short-tempered and the illness isn't really to "blame"?

Since I was a child, my family's nickname for me was "The Bear." I could be moody and uncommunicative when I came downstairs in the morning, unready to talk until I had some breakfast in me, like a bear who had just been roused after hibernation and needed some time or food to become its true self. I would mutter one word in my mother's direction: *cereal.* My older brother, Kevin, whom I idolized, would be at the kitchen table talking a mile a minute. My older sister, Colleen, my greatest confidante, tended to be quiet. You could say I was quiet, too, but grumpier—not angry, but grumpy. Irritable, quick to snap back at you. It was mostly a morning thing, at least when I was younger. I wouldn't talk to or look at anyone until I finished eating. Years later, my parents confessed that they often felt as if they were walking on eggshells around me. Mom said they chalked it up to moodiness. Most of the time I would snap out of it—whatever "it" was—and be just fine. Normal.

Later, when I looked back at how things unraveled, and what I learned from it, I sometimes wondered which reactions and aspects of my behavior were wired to be part of my personality, the "real" me, and which parts were something else, chemistry that went amiss. I came to understand that, no, you can't separate it out like that.

It's all you.

And over time, one of the most interesting revelations I had about the illness was that I didn't *want* to separate it out from the rest of me. I would be losing an important part of what made me me.

Can you imagine if we thought about our body the way we sometimes do about our mind and personality? *No, the upper half of my body—barrel-chested and broad-shouldered— that's not really who I am. My lean legs and flat feet are the "real" me.*

Yeah, no. The bear is a bear when it wakes up from a long sleep and it's a bear two hours later and two months later.

It's always a bear.

Years later, one therapist tried to make me feel better, telling me that I *could* separate out certain unpleasant facets of my life. Soon after I was diagnosed with bipolar I disorder,

I was sitting in her office, still trying to absorb the condition and especially the new label, not wanting to believe it because it sounded so . . . *defining*.

"It can't be true," I fretted. "What am I gonna do? I can't believe I'm bipolar!"

She cut me off. She was a comforting presence—warm brown eyes, nice smile. "Keith, you aren't bipolar. You *have* bipolar. There's a difference. If you had cancer, you wouldn't say, 'I am cancer.' You'd say, 'I have cancer.' You are not bipolar. You have bipolar."

What she said made sense at the time. It also made me feel more relaxed, better about the diagnosis and about myself. Made me feel that bipolar disorder was just an illness. It did not define me.

Yet what she told me, I eventually figured out, was simply not true—at least in my case. Probably not true for lots of other people, as well. My disease was much more than just something I *had*.

~

For most of my life, the one thing that *did* define me, and my family, was football.

August 26, 1980, means two things in the O'Neil household. For one, it's the day my dad, Ed, got cut from the New England Patriots. It ended my father's playing career, which included captaining Penn State's undefeated 1973 team, getting picked eighth in the 1974 NFL Draft by the Detroit Lions, then playing six seasons with them (they were pretty much a .500 team until their terrible 2–14 final season he was there) and one more with the Green Bay Packers. He did not miss a game for the first six and a half seasons in the league, after which injuries started coming one after the other: dislocated shoulder, badly sprained knee, herniated disc. Like almost everyone who plays football that hard, that long, he tried to play a little longer—in his case, with the Pats. He didn't make it. The legendary Bill Parcells, then the team's linebacker coach, cut him on August 26, 1980.

That was also the day I was born.

I grew up in Howell, New Jersey, where my dad had a job at Rutgers University, coaching linebackers, special teams, and tight ends. Growing up in a football family was different. It felt special, magical. Fall weekends were almost always spent at games. Hanging out at stadiums, including Giants Stadium, where the Scarlet Knights played a couple of games a year. Walking around on that field as a kid, sometimes as ball boy—it was an American boy's dream. Being the son of an NFL first-round draft pick and All-America linebacker at Penn State was like being the child of a celebrity, at least in Howell. Everyone in school or at Little League, especially their parents, knew who my dad was. I bragged about it. I brought his football card to school.

His job was high-profile and also highly insecure, which made our close family maybe a little too close. We five knew how uncertain things were, that they could change at the end of any season. I don't think there are that many professions, outside of a family-run business, where the whole family can be so involved in the parent's job. During the season, Dad was rarely around during the week. In the offseason, except for July when we'd all go camping together, he was mostly away on high school recruiting trips. But fall weekends, especially when Rutgers had a home game, we were all there on Saturday afternoon, as regular a routine as church together on Sunday.

Football defined not just the structure of our life but also, in a way, the mentality. Dad went right from finishing his playing career to coaching. Like most football coaches I know, he lived and breathed it—and loved it, too. You have to: Given the level of dedication, the sheer number of hours you put in, you'd better like what you're doing. Hopefully you even love it. So of course football shaped his worldview. Years later, he would leave Rutgers to coach in Buffalo (at the University at Buffalo), then in Germany at Frankfurt and Düsseldorf (for the now-defunct NFL Europe), then in Canada, at Hamilton and Toronto (the Canadian Football League), then back to Buffalo (high school) before retiring. My brother Kevin (who would go on to play football at Syracuse University), my brother-in-law Drew, a star college player played five years in the NFL, and I would joke about buying my father a football-shaped globe because his world *was* football. My mom says he always finds a way to bring the conversation back to football. "Dad," I could say, "I don't understand this new knee fixation device I'm selling at work and how to use it properly."

"Well, Keith," Dad might answer, "It's like the Cover 2 (a defensive coverage). The more you do it, the more you'll understand it."

In our house, football was life.

And life was mostly normal, even idyllic. We had a white picket fence and a black Lab named Paddy. We lived in a modest three-bedroom Colonial, with light blue aluminum siding, on a corner lot. Behind us were woods with several big holes in the ground, almost pits, perfect for building forts and playing army and manhunt. There was an above-ground pool and a big climbing tree in the middle of the backyard. We played football in the side-yard with other neighborhood kids. Sometimes we played it in the schoolyard across the street. Games always broke out. When I played—usually with boys several years older, because most of them were Kevin's friends and they always needed an extra player—I never backed down. I liked the competition. I would pretend I was my dad. We played football indoors, too: The back of the house, the family room, was where we did most of our playing—Legos, Nintendo, etc.—and my absolute favorite thing was to come home from Rutgers games on Saturday nights and Kevin and I would go straight to the family room, take all the cushions off the couches, put them over the "pointy" furniture, and play football. Because of our age difference, he played on his knees and I played standing up. Our background music was Saturday night college football games on TV.

Mom was the backbone of the family, holding everything together while Dad was at work and out of town for chunks of time. A good parent puts her kids in a position to succeed, just like a good coach puts his players in a position to succeed. That was Mom, guiding us but also giving us freedom.

Even though I could be The Bear (at least until I had a couple bowls of cereal in me), I was also thought of as a caring, sweet kid—at least for a while. I was not the greatest student, a dreamer frequently off in my own world, but Mom did her best to help me study. My teachers liked me. So did my extended family, especially my aunts. I collected baseball cards and football cards. I excelled at sports, especially baseball. I loved music. I was an altar boy at our local parish, St. Veronica's. Normal stuff.

But there was other stuff, too. Was it normal? Typical little boy stuff, or something else? When does behavior become a "sign" of something and not just who you *really* are, or just a normal stage you're going through?

You are always who you are.

In second grade, two weeks before my first communion, I spray-painted *Fuck You* on the houses of several neighbors.

Occasionally I bullied kids. I liked to fight, especially with kids my brother's age—four years older—because I wanted to prove myself. In third grade, I got into an argument with a boy in Kevin's class. I threw the first punch. I remember how proud Kevin was. I got in huge trouble for it, of course, but even Mom couldn't get completely angry with me when the boy's mother called to complain how I was at fault because I'd thrown the first punch. What my mother *wanted* to say was, "Lady, your son is four years older than mine." She didn't, though.

It was not the only fight I got into in third and fourth grade.

Okay, you're probably forming an opinion of me.

I thought I was a good kid, just a little mischievous. As far as I could tell, no one in my family thought I was a bad child, a delinquent. Like I said, I could be sweet and caring, and most of the time I was. Everyone brushed off my occasional antics. I mooned a girl. I set some small fires and egged some houses and broke a few windows. Pretty standard for a lot of little boys growing up in the suburbs, right?

Or was it a sign of something else, like impulse control problems? Or the need to feel that rush of adrenaline?

By age eight, something else started happening: I was feeling anxiety, particularly about falling asleep. Upstairs were three bedrooms—one for my parents, one for Colleen, one for Kevin and me. He and I had a bunk bed, me on the top. Our walls were covered with sports posters, happy things to dream about. But my mind just wouldn't, couldn't shut off. Why? I had a warm bed, a loving family, a safe house and neighborhood. My parents had a strong marriage. Mom ran a daycare from home to help make ends meet while also being around her own kids. Amazingly, given what Dad did for work, we even had stability. (He had turned down at least one "better" coaching job while we lived in New Jersey so we didn't have to move.) I had a sister I could tell everything to and a brother I worshipped.

It didn't matter. Even though my siblings and the neighborhood kids and I played after school until we dropped, it still didn't help. I dreaded bedtime. Since I was younger than Kevin, I would go to bed first but I would lie there, eyes open, staring at the ceiling, waiting for him, sometimes for hours. It didn't matter if Mom came in to help by lying down with me or talking to me or cuddling with me or getting mad at me. My mind was occupied by thoughts of things that were going to happen the next day. Anticipating, worrying. But lots of kids do that, right? And most of them grow out of it, right?

And it wasn't as if I worried about everything. I didn't worry about making friends. I didn't worry about excelling at sports. I worried about . . . well, I worried about everything else.

My very Catholic father saw that I was struggling. "Maybe we should put a Bible in your pillowcase?" he suggested. So we put a pocket Bible in my pillowcase.

Yeah, that didn't help.

We had always prayed as a family, before meals and bedtime, but now, because of my anxiety, I started to pray on my own. If my parents couldn't help me with my sleep problem, who else could I go to? A higher power, naturally. My father was raised Catholic, my mother Christian, and we attended church every Sunday at St. Veronica's. To get through church I daydreamed (I know I'm not alone in that). While we never opened the Bible as a family, and at home we weren't taught scripture, just Catholic prayer, I was exposed to God and religion at a young age.

Now I needed God to help me sleep. He didn't answer but I didn't give up: I had no Plan B. By the time I was ten or eleven, I started frequently to lock myself in the upstairs bathroom, the one we three kids shared, and light candles and pray for sleep. Small candles, lots of them, all around the edge of the bathtub, and a bunch more on the floor. I would sit on the (closed) toilet seat and just think and mostly pray about sleeping. Sometimes I noticed the moon in the window and would focus on that. I often wore headphones and listened to music, mostly grunge—Pearl Jam, Nirvana, others. I might stay in the locked bathroom for a half-hour.

That helped about as much as the pocket Bible in my pillowcase. My problems with sleep only got worse. I had enough religion to believe that things happen for a reason, and my sleeplessness made no sense to me. I could not understand why my prayers went unanswered.

Every now and then, a suicidal thought crept in.

I sometimes stared into my parents' bathroom cabinet at all the medications, and thought about how taking lots of them all at once might kill me. Even the linen closet made me think: It's where Mom kept the rubbing alcohol and peroxide. If I drank both bottles, I was pretty certain they would kill me. No, definitely they would. These were just thoughts, though.

Okay, I was a depressed little kid—at least some of the time.

And maybe being depressed like that is normal.

More than anything, though, I felt different. I felt things more deeply than I suspected other people did. Was I actually, technically depressed? I don't know. My paternal grandfather, Howdo, had depression and mood swings, though it's not as if I recognized myself in him. My dad would tell me how Howdo was either the life of the party or locked in a room upstairs sleeping. How he would talk your ear off or just not talk at all. There was no "open secret" in the family about Howdo's behavior, some idea that he could not function. He was a workingman, with a full-time job at an electrical company in northwest Pennsylvania, and a side business cleaning rugs to make ends meet. It was hard for those around him to say that he had some kind of mental disorder. Back then, bad or good, you went about your business.

At school, I struggled academically. I would call myself a very average student. The teachers never had problems with my behavior. The only time my parents sought special help was in second grade, when I had trouble pronouncing certain consonants, especially the letter "r." "Girl" would sound like "gull." I got past it in a semester.

My most reliable refuge was sports. Everyone in my family played them, loved competing at them, usually starred at them. Kevin was a phenomenal athlete, probably better all-around than me, though in the end maybe not a better football player. He was faster and better at track and basketball, while I was better at baseball. He and I always competed hard *against* each other, the way athletic brothers do, and I sometimes looked to provoke him. But we weren't competitive *with* each other and I didn't compare myself to him, though maybe it sounds as if I am. Kevin eventually went to Syracuse University, a top Division I-A school, to play linebacker. An amazing achievement. I wanted to play Division I-A college football someday—Michigan, Syracuse, even Rutgers, where Dad coached, even if they usually didn't do all that well record-wise.

My sister Colleen, nineteen months older than me, was the best athlete of us all. As a pole vaulter, she was the first in the state of New Jersey to clear the opening height as a sophomore. She was a pentathlete, great at sprints, high jump, long jump, and hurdles. She was a district champion. She broke many school records. As a cheerleader, her squad competed at the national level.

As I said, despite the uncertainty built into a football career, we were lucky to have a stable family life. After my father had been at Rutgers for six years, the head coach was fired and a new one was brought in—yet still my dad was kept on. He was well liked. A year or two went by and he was obviously a valued member of the new staff. It wasn't the usual way things happened, though. Almost all the coaches I've known have been all over the country, criss-crossing it like someone's chasing them. They move their families from place to place, hot after their dream of someday becoming head coach somewhere, preferably a big school. That kind of mentality puts a lot of stress on the family. My linebacker coach with the Dallas Cowboys made his home in Texas while his family lived in another state. When I was younger, I thought that was a pretty selfish way to live, but that was probably because we hadn't had to, for a good long time. Why, I wondered, don't they just get a high school football coaching job, teach gym, and live with their wife and kids?

By middle school, my fleeting suicidal thoughts were in check. My anxiety and insomnia were somewhat in check. My moodiness was not. Maybe it's who I was.

I had more and more trouble concentrating in school, especially when I wasn't interested in the subject or it got a little too complex (which naturally made me lose interest). Luckily, I could bullshit my way through. Occasionally I'd cheat. But I was also smart, though maybe more street-smart than school-smart.

Then again, to thrive as a kid, especially a boy, it can really help to have athletic success. My father, who never pressured my brother and me to follow in his footsteps, did not allow us to play organized football until eighth grade. But the moment I could sign up for Pop Warner, got put on the Howell Lions, and was made a starter on both defense and offense, it was clear that I had the instincts and genes for the game. My speed enabled me to star at football (as running back and linebacker), track (sprints), and lacrosse (midfielder). (I gave up baseball to play lacrosse.) I didn't think of myself as a dumb jock. I didn't hang out with any sort of football crowd. I smoked some weed. I had friends. I had girlfriends. Things were good. I enjoyed being a football star.

Chapter 2

I-A

The bubble burst.

For a football coach at the college or pro level, my father had managed an amazingly stable life for us growing up, one highly difficult to replicate: an entire decade in the same place. Your kids grow up in one house, keep their friends and their identity at school, go to sleep each night in *their* bed.

But it was time. He felt he had been at Rutgers long enough, through multiple regimes, and so he resigned. At age forty-two, for the first time in a decade, he had to look for employment. He took a job at Freehold Township High School, one town over from Howell, as gym teacher and head football coach. Then, after a year there, he got a call from the University at Buffalo about an opening as defensive coordinator—one notch below (along with offensive coordinator) head coach.

The move to western New York was extremely difficult on me. I left behind my childhood friends and memories, from nursery school through eighth grade. Selfishly but not surprisingly for a fourteen-year-old, I did not focus on how lucky I had had it up to then, a football coach's son, but on what I was losing. I was established in New Jersey. I was excited to enter high school there, where my brother and sister had starred at sports and paved the way for me, with all kinds of high expectations for who I was and what I could do and how I might also help fill the trophy case in the lobby of Howell High School. I *liked* being Keith O'Neil, kid brother of Kevin and Colleen. That's who I'd been all my life.

Now I had to start over in Buffalo. Lost, with no real identity. We were moving too far away to keep in touch with old friends, or even hope to visit them on weekends. Kevin was off to college, to play for Syracuse. Colleen was dazed. The change was hardest on her and me. Dad was especially busy in his new position so Mom held the pieces together as best she could. We were now a lot closer to Michigan, where she grew up and my grandmother still lived. But it was new territory for all of us.

We arrived in Buffalo in July 1995, with nothing to do. Colleen and I became particularly close that summer. Between us, we had zero friends. It felt as if all we had was each other. All we did was rollerblade together around the big, quiet neighborhood.

Our house in Buffalo was larger than the one in suburban New Jersey because our new town was more affordable. We had a porch that reached from the garage all the way to the other end of the house, and an in-ground pool. I turned fifteen a month after we arrived and had more freedom than ever. I know, it sounds as if I didn't have much to complain about. But Colleen, a high school junior, found a way to skip school almost every day, which was sad because in New Jersey she had had so many friends and was such a star athlete. In Buffalo, she wanted nothing to do with her new crowd, so she just checked out. She was a ghost at Sweet Home High School.

And high school football in western New York—sorry to say this—was a joke. At least it was in 1995 and the four years I lived there. In Jersey, everyone in town came out for the local games. In Buffalo, we had no support. The talent level was thin. After making junior varsity as a starter my freshman year, I almost immediately hurt my shoulder in the first game of the season after a particularly hard collision with the opposing fullback. I missed three games, the only games I would miss during my high school career.

Once the school year started, I made friends pretty fast, including Jimmy, to this day the smartest person I know, and Paul, the biggest-hearted, most fun guy I had ever met. But my anxiety began to creep back—along with the insomnia. To this day, I hate the call of mourning doves: Their sad, drawn-out, pleading sounds remind me of the nightly call of the mourning doves of my adolescence, and how it was like a countdown. *Almost bedtime. Time to try to fall asleep.* (Cue sound of doves.)

Same with the theme songs of certain TV shows: *Cheers, Unsolved Mysteries, Rescue 911, Monday Night Football.* Sure, I liked watching them but the music was a warning. My nightly struggle with sleep was coming up fast.

Throughout high school I dealt with bouts of depression, but nothing substantial—or maybe I mean nothing *noticeable.*

If you had asked my friends and other students who knew me, I'm sure they wouldn't have remarked on anything about my behavior that would be considered unusual. (But maybe that's because, like most teens, they were completely focused on themselves.) Plus, I was captain of the football team. I had girlfriends. I was popular. What was there to be depressed about? What teenager wouldn't want that life? Of course, just because people don't notice you're feeling something doesn't mean you're not feeling something. My grandpa Howdo held two jobs and supported a family and was sometimes the life of the party, and he was going through something. Was mine a "real," clinical depression or the kind of "depression" so prevalent among high school kids that maybe we don't think of it as quite real, though it most certainly is to the individual experiencing it? At that age, I never experienced mania or even hypomania: a milder, often enjoyable and constructive form of mania. I lived a pretty normal high school life, or as normal as it gets when you're captain of the football team. I had a normal high school job, making breadsticks at Olive Garden (though I quit after a month from the monotony). I got a job at the Buffalo Shooting Club, a trap and skeet club, keeping score for the shooters or sitting in the trap house loading clay pigeons into the machines. I'm pretty sure I was not on anyone's "bizarre behavior" radar—not even my own. Having occasional trouble falling asleep is not exactly breaking news.

As for football: I dreaded practice. First, because I often had physical pain, especially shin splints, but also because I was just—is there a nicer way to say this about myself?—lazy. (I'm not sure if it helped or hurt me that I was naturally strong, and weightlifting wasn't something I had to work at that hard.) Now, was this laziness a result of depression, or an aspect of my personality that can't be "written off" to mental illness? I never felt motivated to get excited about practice or even to fake acting excited about it—but when I *did* practice, which was all the time, I practiced hard, and each time it was over I felt an incredible sense of well-being, both physically and mentally. There's a rush of endorphins that contributes to that. Knowing I would end up at that place, spent and with a sense of accomplishment, got me through the drudgery and pain. The physical exertion and chemical release probably helped my mental state. I literally sweated out my stress and anxiety.

~

Junior year, when big colleges really start recruiting top high school talent, I was getting zero attention, even though I was a star at my school and had made a name in the area. In our region, Sweet Home High was a good football team, not great. And it didn't help my recruiting chances that I wasn't doing very well academically. My parents told me that unless I brought up my grades, I couldn't play my spring sport, lacrosse, which I loved. They hired a tutor. I took a Kaplan course at the University at Buffalo to help me test better. I brought up my scores and got to play lacrosse, but it may have been too little too late for the better schools.

I attended football camp at Rutgers and hoped to impress the coaches there with my speed and talent, but I guess they didn't like what they saw. I had always dreamed of playing at a big school—Michigan, Oregon, Penn State, Florida, anyplace major would have made me happy. It will come as no surprise that as a child, before I dreamed of playing at any of those prestigious colleges, I most wanted to play for Rutgers, where my dad coached. I occasionally ball-boyed for them and looked up to the players on the squad, fantasizing that someday I would be a Scarlet Knight. It didn't matter that they were usually so-so and often pretty terrible: They were still Division I-A, the top level of college football. Kevin and I often talked about it, daydreaming and scheming. Together, the two O'Neil Brothers were going to make Rutgers matter. Someday.

"The O'Neil Boys Save the Day" seemed a pipe dream, mostly mine, because Kevin could have gone anywhere to play—and eventually did, at Syracuse. And football camp wasn't bringing any attention for me.

But I was determined to show them—whoever "they" were. For one, because of an injury, I still hadn't played my best. Now, any serious athlete plays with pain of some sort, at all times. I suffered from bad shin splints, which started during two-a-day practices before my freshman year and dogged me for more than two years, through football, indoor track, and lacrosse, though I never missed time because of them. But with almost every step I was in pain. I tried orthotics. I tried physical therapy. I took lots of ibuprofen. Finally, in spring of my junior year, I had a surgical procedure called a fasciotomy: The fascia, the sheath of tissue that surrounds the muscle, is cut, relieving pressure and restoring circulation to an area of tissue or muscle. I was on crutches for a couple weeks but made a quick recovery. It was a game-changer for me, I thought.

That summer, right before senior year, I again attended football camp: at Ann Arbor, on the campus of the University of Michigan.

Once again, I made no impact. Maybe it was that I was "just" six feet tall, or that my grades and test scores were not great. The dream of playing big-college football, a part of the puzzle I needed to fill if I was to realize my bigger dream of playing in the NFL, was beginning to fade: Even Rutgers appeared uninterested—or, I should say, they were interested until they weren't. They sent me a couple letters—generic ones, with questionnaires to fill out your height, weight, position, etc. Nothing personal from a coach. But then even the form letters stopped. No other big schools were interested.

When "Signing Day" came and went without a big-time offer, something that both my brother and future brother-in-law had received, I was devastated.

Senior year, I had my first offer: the University of Maine, a Division I-AA school. (That's a clear notch below I-A.) I didn't know at the time that this would make up exactly half of all the offers I would get. No, not even Rutgers—shitty Rutgers!—offered me a scholarship.

My last season of high school football ended without fanfare—we didn't even make the playoffs. So that was it? Go to Maine and play for them or try to make it elsewhere as a walk-on? Virtually no one at the really big schools are walk-ons, plus it means you're paying for college, which would have been a significant burden on my parents.

Colleen, my confidante, had left home to start at the University at Buffalo and lived in a dorm there, but she was home many weekends, often accompanied by her boyfriend, Drew Haddad, a sophomore star wide receiver for UB. I needed their support. I broke down.

"I can't believe I'm not even good enough for Rutgers— shitty Rutgers!" I cried. How unrealistic were my football aspirations if a college team as bad as they didn't want me?

It helped having Drew there: He could offer perspective. He had been a very, very good high school football player, probably better than I was, and had attended a high school with a far better-respected football program than mine:

national powerhouse Saint Ignatius in Cleveland, Ohio. And with all that, he got just one Division I-A scholarship offer.

But Drew's case wasn't even the one that gave me perspective, sobering as it was to consider. It was Drew's older brother, Eric, whose story I also needed to learn from. Eric, a running back, had been a huge football star in football-crazed Ohio, and when he was at St. Ignatius before Drew, they were *the* top high school football team in the country. He set all kinds of school records. One season, he scored 33 touchdowns. He went to Purdue University, in the Big Ten conference, on a full scholarship . . . and never played his freshman year. The head coach changed and they switched their offensive schemes, from two running backs in most backfield sets to just one. As a fullback, he was the dispensable one. Sophomore year, he carried the ball twice. Junior year, he started once, touching the ball eight times the entire season. Senior year, he started twice. And that was it. The end of his football career.

Eric's younger brother Drew was three years older than me and I looked up to him, as I looked up to Kevin. Drew would sometimes say about himself and me, "We're the younger brothers of high school heroes." That motivated me. He also used to say, "You can't measure heart with a stop watch." Our brothers were faster than we were—but not necessarily better football players.

Perspective is fine. But I was still supremely bummed.

Guess I was going to Maine.

In December, my high school guidance counselor called me into his office. He said a coach from Northern Arizona University was coming to school to talk to me at three o'clock that afternoon. Until that moment, I had never heard of Northern Arizona University. I had the one standing scholarship offer from Maine. Glad as I was to have that in hand, I wasn't sure how excited I was to go from playing football in my adopted hometown of Buffalo to northern, equally frigid Maine. So I was psyched for my meeting.

But an hour after the NAU coach had promised to be there, he hadn't shown. I walked home from school through the grey, snowy, darkening Buffalo afternoon, feeling like a nobody: Someone from a school I had never heard of had stood me up. Those who were disappointed in me (if they were) had a right to be. I had a huge sense of disappointment in myself, especially for not getting a single Division I-A offer. Turned out I was not going to be like my dad or brother.

The instant I walked into the house, the phone rang. It was my guidance counselor. He said the NAU coach had finally shown up, really, and I needed to come back as fast as I could. I jumped into my brother's car and sped back to school.

When I met Cliff Schwenke, NAU's defensive line coach, he asked me, "Where did you picture yourself at this point in the recruiting process?"

"I thought I would be going to Michigan or Penn State, like my father, or Syracuse, like my brother," I replied, not savvy enough to say nice things about his institution. "But I'm not."

"Well, we'd like you to come out to visit our school," he said. A visit, not a scholarship. But hey, it was something.

It was strange to me that he was even there. I mean, what was a coach from Arizona doing at Sweet Home High School in Amherst, New York? I asked him.

He said he was a "back East" guy who was home attending to "family matters" and decided to do a little recruiting while he was back. He stopped by St. Francis High School, one of the local powerhouses, to ask their head coach his opinion of the local talent. And *their* coach told him about me.

It's always nice to have people say good things about you, maybe even nicer when it's people you don't know. But I also couldn't help but wonder: What if Coach Schwenke had not been visiting his family? This meeting was the result of random circumstance, I thought, not anything I had controlled the way I went to football camps and tried to make the coaches there recognize my value.

By the time my parents and I got on the plane out to Arizona for the visit, NAU informed us that there was a full scholarship waiting for me . . . if I wanted.

We weren't even halfway on the drive from Phoenix, where we landed, to Flagstaff, where the campus was located, when I turned to my father and said, under my breath, "I'm coming here." (Could I be impulsive? Yes.) It almost didn't matter what Flagstaff looked like but it was beautiful nonetheless, and I fell in love with it immediately. And how impulsive was I being, anyway? No offense to Maine, but I didn't ever really want to go there, yet I hadn't let myself express that when their offer was the only one on the table.

Now I was determined to make the best of my situation. I had a four-year scholarship to a school in the middle of gorgeous Arizona. They clearly wanted me. I could truly enjoy the last few months of high school. Even my sleeping issues and anxiety seemed to be in check, maybe because I knew what was happening next.

Or maybe my "issues" were just hibernating, and would come to life eventually.

After all, I was The Bear.

Chapter 3

ME VS. WORLD (OTHERS, TRAINS, MYSELF, ETC.)

I arrived in Flagstaff two weeks before school and football season started to begin working out. It was too early to move into the dorms so the coaching staff set me up with another incoming freshman, C.R. Duley, whose dad, Ed, had also played football at NAU, then briefly in the pros for the Houston Oilers. I don't know if C.R. and I hit it off because we both had dads named Ed who played in the NFL or for all the other reasons we liked each other, but we got along from the start. I loved his family. They had a vacation home nearby and right away took me in and treated me like one of their own, making my homesickness a little more bearable.

(I wasn't the only one feeling the distance: Mom told me much later that even though she saw how nice Arizona was and how much I liked NAU, her heart dropped over how far away it was.)

At practice, I could tell pretty quickly that I had more talent than almost everyone there. I was faster and stronger than even the upperclassmen. As a Division I-AA school, NAU gave out about twenty fewer scholarships than Division I-A schools like Syracuse and Michigan, which meant that there were fewer scholarship-caliber players to line up next to and compete for playing time against, and also that a good chunk of the rest of the team wasn't on scholarship. Within the division, my new school was okay with a chance to be better than that. When I got time in an actual game, which didn't happen all that much as a freshman, I played well. Problem was, though I had been bypassed by all the name schools, as well as schools a level below the name schools, I had not given up my dream to play beyond college, and it's much, much harder to get noticed at a small school and get drafted from there. Then again, I had more chance to play at a smaller school. I thought of Eric, Drew's star running back brother at big-time Purdue.

Some of the older players on the team started to call me "League": They saw my talent and thought I could actually make it to the National Football League. It was a real compliment. I had another natural nickname: KO, given to me by my linebacker coach, Greg Lees. Yes, they were my initials, but the name also seemed to fit, given how hard I hit.

And there was the old standby nickname: My roommates and closest friends and teammates, who witnessed my moods firsthand, sometimes called me The Bear. It didn't bother me.

They chose a football player for me to live with in the freshman dorm, with C.R. and another football player down the hall. Since C.R. and I had already become close and liked to party together, we wanted to share a room. One afternoon, while C.R.'s roommate was out studying, we just moved all of his stuff into my room, then my stuff into C.R.'s, without asking. When his roommate came back to see that he had been displaced and he was now C.R.'s ex-roommate, he was pissed. He told C.R. and me to fuck off. It blew over.

Several teammates, including one of my dormmates and eventual best friends, Ka'aina Keawe, were Polynesian, from Hawaii, and there were also many Samoan and Tongan players I grew close to. Ka'aina and the other Polynesians taught me the meaning of *ohana* (family), and joked that I was a crazy *haole* (someone not native Hawaiian, particularly a white person) from New York.

To fit in, I realized, I didn't need a big football program or fraternity scene or bar scene. That would have just got me into trouble. Going to NAU, I felt, was the best decision of my life. I didn't need Michigan or Penn State.

Part of it was that I fell in love with Flagstaff and the surrounding areas, like Sedona and the Grand Canyon. NAU sits at the base of the San Francisco Peaks, a stunning mountain range. C.R. and I would often take out four-wheelers and cruise through the northern Arizona pines. And the town itself was beautiful and laid-back, very liberal—even hippie—completely different from Buffalo and New Jersey and exactly what I needed: tranquility. Gigantic blue sky. The smell of Ponderosa pine. A million stars at night. During football practice, I often found myself staring at the mountains ringing the campus when I should have been paying attention.

Still, I was also down a lot. Everything seemed to be a struggle. I worked extremely hard at my academics yet I was not motivated—if that makes sense. I was mostly a C student, particularly struggling in math and science, though I got As in my health courses, like First Aid/CPR and Athletic Training, and Bs in creative writing and history. When I would call home, which sometimes happened several times a day, I talked mostly with Colleen or my mom, and the anxiety would spill out.

I can't be this far away from home, I would complain.

This place is so different.

The football program isn't that good.

They're not playing me enough.

Often I just wanted to go home. I missed my friends—well, not so much missed them as the comfort of them, the idea of them.

Much later, when I became a devoted reader of bipolar magazines (yes, there are quite a few), I learned that going to college and the stress that goes with it, as well as the loss of the familiar "scaffolding" of parental support, is a trigger for lots of people. (The stresses of being a student-athlete in high school don't compare to being a scholarship athlete in college.)

Despite my love of Flagstaff and its beauty, I constantly thought of quitting. In fact, the dramatic difference in my surroundings might have been more of a jolt than I could handle. Once, C.R. and I found ourselves on four-wheelers, out in the middle of nature, the mountains and buttes rising up, the gorgeous valleys and peaks, and suddenly we were riding next to a herd of galloping elk . . . and rather than appreciating the moment for what it was, just being in the present, all I kept thinking was: *How the hell did I get here? Where the fuck am I?*

If it weren't for C.R. and the Duleys and Ka'aina and some other valued friends, I probably would have transferred back home and attended college somewhere near Buffalo. Maybe I could go to a school closer to home that would want me, like Edinboro University of Pennsylvania, a Division II school, or Buffalo State, Division III. They would both take me in a second.

But I didn't know how to quit.

~

Maybe I didn't think I needed a bar scene, but I drank a lot while at NAU. C.R. and I were party buddies. We ran around Flagstaff and the clubs in nearby, bigger Scottsdale. We partied a lot. I needed it to cope. Alcohol helped me escape reality, which was really a synonym for stress, or vice versa. The more liquor, the better. The more risk, the more I was drawn to it. Whatever stresses I experienced in college were now "successfully" masked by my drinking and the haven of football—the focus of it and the violence. When I drank, I got into fights. My fuse got short fast, especially with whiskey. I was a mean drunk. I was impulsive, I blacked out. I felt invincible and tough. I didn't *think* I was looking for a fight, but if you did anything to my girlfriend, my friend, or me, I was ready to kick your ass. It was fun for me. I was fearless. Not that I won all the fights. Once, I played in a playoff game with a broken nose from getting sucker-punched at a bar, a sucker punch I totally deserved.

You don't need a lot of bars to get into trouble. NAU had three or four main hangouts, nothing compared to Arizona State University in Tempe, with three times as many students and a reputation—not just in Arizona but among American colleges, generally—for its party scene.

Which effect of drinking drew me most? The escaping of reality, the "opening" up, the confidence boost? I really couldn't say. I knew I was drawn to adrenaline rushes. Ka'aina and I would take turns driving 130 mph down Interstate 40 in Flagstaff in my 1998 silver Camaro, the one my parents promised they'd buy me if I got a scholarship.

But how was this a sign of mental illness? Or a "split personality"? If you're nineteen and playing football at a beautiful spot in the desert and you have a badass Camaro, wouldn't *you* do the same?

During my freshman year, I played special teams and some backup linebacker, probably more than most freshman would because the guy ahead of me had a bad shoulder. I always did my job on the field. My coaches and teammates and, I hope, every opponent could always see I was never at sea.

Off the field, I admit it: I was no prince. I continued to drink a lot, get into fights, and do really stupid things. St. Patrick's Day of that year, I had way too much to drink (go figure). My friends and I decided to walk home from the bars, which meant crossing the train tracks. At a certain point, I stopped to take a piss behind a dumpster. By the time I finished, my friends had already crossed the tracks and the mechanical crossing guard was down. I jogged to catch up to them, edged my way past the wooden guard, stepped onto the tracks, and started walking on them until I turned to see the train coming right at me.

And I was blind drunk.

I began jumping and yelling at the train. I was not playing chicken with it but I probably seemed a bit too casual in stepping off the track just seconds before the train shot by.

I walked back onto the road and continued down the street, unaware that a policeman in his cruiser had stopped when the guards went down and saw the whole episode. So when he pulled up beside me and asked for my ID, I did not know what it was about. To me, it seemed a long time since the train tracks. I handed him my brother's ID, which I used for drinking purposes (Kevin was twenty-three, I was nineteen), and the cop brought me back to the police station, where I took a Breathalyzer test and blew an out-of-control .28. "Highly intoxicated" is an understatement. I was charged with trespassing, underage consumption, and false identification. They locked me up. For my one allowed call, I phoned Colleen. I remember the operator saying to her, "You have a collect call from the Coconino County Jail"—and remember nothing else from our conversation. Then I was in a room with a dozen cots. I guess I passed out. A few hours later I was released when my good friend Trent, who had been with me the night before, came to bail me out.

Two days later, the front-page headline of the local newspaper read "Taking On A Train." As I was reading the story in my dorm room, the phone rang. It was the NAU compliance director. She knew and liked me, but she had a job to do.

"Please tell me your middle name doesn't start with the letter D," she said, hopefully. "Because the story in the paper says a Keith D. O'Neil was arrested."

"Yeah, sorry," I said, sheepishly. "It's Daniel."

She told me to come down to the football complex to talk with the athletic director and head coach. The AD lectured me, as he had every right. My coach was more disappointed than angry. Still, school policy stipulated that if you're arrested, you automatically go on "investigative suspension," which meant I could not compete in any practices or games until my case was settled.

In the end, I was suspended for only three days. I paid a fine for underage consumption, false identification, and third-degree trespassing. I was back playing spring ball by the end of the week.

Like my coach, my parents were both understanding and disappointed. When I told them about it I stretched the truth: In that version, I crossed under the rail guards as they were going down, and that was all. I never walked on the tracks or acted like an idiot as the train approached. And since they knew I had my brother's fake ID and went to bars, they couldn't get that upset if the story ended there. They kind of let it go.

My teammates made a joke of it. The rest of the spring, when the upperclassmen saw me at practice, they would chant, "Choo-choo, choo-choo!" Since I was still a freshman, I just took it.

C.R. transferred to ASU after our freshman year. True, they had better parties. But NAU was just too small for him, and the legend of his father, Ed, who had starred there on his way to a brief career in the NFL, was always present. Even though C.R. was a hell of a player himself, he just didn't want to play football anymore.

Not that my drinking stopped after C.R. transferred. On a Thursday night during my sophomore year, Ka'aina and some other teammates and I went out to the bars and got ripped. The next day we had to travel to Los Angeles to play Cal State Northridge. I was still so drunk that I didn't really wake up until we got off the buses in LA. I hadn't brought a thing—no pillow, change of clothes, toothbrush, scouting report. It was all I could do just to get myself on the bus in time. When we returned to Flagstaff and I got back to the dorm complex, I couldn't find my car. My friends and I searched and searched. Finally, a neighbor told me that it had been towed because it was parked in the middle of the grass in front of the apartment.

~

I made a good impression with my play freshman year, then occasionally started sophomore year, splitting time with another sophomore linebacker. My junior year, I thought, would be my breakout season. They wouldn't hold me back anymore, the way they often do with freshmen and even sophomores, in favor of juniors or seniors who are higher on the depth chart sometimes just because they're juniors or seniors.

Then, just as preseason began, I learned that a highly-rated junior college transfer was coming to NAU to play the exact position I played. And he wasn't coming to be the backup.

Besides upsetting me, the news confused me: Why would they bring in a transfer to start in front of me, when I was the fastest, strongest—and yes, best—linebacker on the team, if not the whole conference? And even if they liked this transfer, how could they not want to find a place for me on the field? I didn't want to see it as favoritism but it seemed that the defensive coordinator, who was Polynesian, preferred the many Polynesian players on the team (many of whom were among our best players), and the new transfer was also Polynesian. The position coach who had recruited me to come to NAU was long gone, and typically the guy who recruits you pulls for you. I was the kid from New York, the only player on the team from "back East." I had no ties to Arizona. No one on the coaching staff seemed to care much whether I started or even played. To them, I was a beer-drinking, ass-kicking white boy who liked bars and got into scrapes with the local police.

I had a huge chip on my shoulder about being passed over—yet I wasn't up to fighting for my spot. Maybe I *was* a quitter. I called my dad to tell him it was time. I was ready to transfer to a smaller school closer to home.

"Stick it out," he advised me. "You never know what will happen." Typical loving parental advice, but I didn't have much faith in his words.

In our first game of the 2001 season, the third play of the game, while I rode the bench, George, the star junior college transfer starting in front of me, broke his leg.

You never know.

As George's "replacement," I played out of my mind all season long. We finished with a record of 8–4 and made the playoffs, where we lost in the first round to Sam Houston State, 34–31. After the season, I was named 1st Team All-Big Sky Conference. I had developed a reputation as a linebacker who could run fast and hit hard. I appreciated that Drew, my sister's boyfriend, continued writing me letters of encouragement, only now from the NFL—he'd been drafted by the Buffalo Bills. It also helped that, even with the distance between Flagstaff and back home, I could almost always count on having at least one family member at each home game. That's what football families do.

Meanwhile, Dad got a job as defensive coordinator with NFL Europe, first for the Rhein Fire and then the Frankfurt Galaxy. He would spend eight seasons in Germany. Mom didn't move with him for the seasons but spent a lot of time over there, traveling back and forth. Kevin, Colleen, and I visited when we could. While Dad was with the Galaxy, they won two World Bowls.

Due to the demands on a college football player's time—practice, film study, conditioning, games, travel—the options for classes were limited. There was a class called "Women in American History" that I would not have thought to take, but it fit my schedule and satisfied one of my academic requirements—and thank God, because the moment I laid eyes on Jill Eddie, a sophomore nursing major from Kingman, Arizona, and one of my classmates (there were about fifty women in the class and five men), I was in love. She had her hair pulled back, and wore a brown leather jacket, and immediately I was caught by her piercing green eyes. By the third class, we were sitting beside each other.

Jill was (and is) the sweetest person I've ever met. Everyone loved her. She never talked bad about people. Unlike me, she thought things through so that she always seemed to make the right decision. And she was smart. She would graduate at the top of her class, *summa cum laude*, with an incredible 4.1 GPA.

I quit drinking, for two reasons: I now had Jill in my life, plus after a great junior year of football and just one more season left to prove myself to the NFL as draft-worthy, I needed to focus and have an even better year.

(I had recently picked up a chewing tobacco habit, but that calmed me rather than riled me up.)

In 2002, my senior season, I again made 1st Team All-Big Sky at linebacker, plus 1st Team All-America (Division I-AA). My last home game in college, the whole family came out to see me play. As the game ended, Colleen stood and held up a sign that read, YOU CAN COME HOME NOW.

For all the accolades, I knew that being from a non-Division I-A school meant it would be a long shot to get drafted by an NFL team. I would need to shine at the NFL scouting combine, the showcase held every year around the beginning of March in Indianapolis, where players are invited to come show off their speed, strength, and football skills in anticipation of the draft two months later. Over Christmas break, I returned to Buffalo and met with the Buffalo Bills' strength and conditioning coach, a friend of my dad's, for advice. He measured my body fat percentage and gave me a diet to follow. Before I headed back to school, I was at a restaurant where I bumped into a guy who'd played football at a rival high school. We had played together in a high school all-star game senior year. We had a friend or two in common. He was a big guy, bigger than me. He asked me what I was doing home.

"Training for the NFL," I said.

He looked me up and down. "Give up the pipe dream," he said.

In preparation for the combine, I got into the best shape of my life. Two months later, when invitations for the combine went out, I got nothing.

~

Greg Lees, my linebacker coach from college, helped me to set up my *own* combine: I would have a "pro day" on our home NAU field, just for me, timing it so that at least some pro scouts could come watch. Drew, who was now with the Indianapolis Colts, also helped me prepare.

In the end, six scouts showed up to see me perform: representatives from the Colts, Jacksonville Jaguars, San Francisco 49ers, Detroit Lions, Kansas City Chiefs, and the expansion Houston Texans. I felt good about what I showed them, doing the 40-yard dash, bench press, vertical jump, broad jump, three-cone drill, 20-yard shuttle, measurements (hands, arms, etc.), and linebacker drills. I approached the draft feeling excited.

~

It was the end of April and my family flew in to Arizona from Buffalo to be with me. Dad couldn't be there because he was coaching in Europe, though I knew how much he wanted to share the draft moment with me.

The NFL Draft used to take two days to complete (now it's over three). If you're a top prospect from a school like Alabama or Ohio State or USC, obviously you go early, on Day 1. For me, it would be a long two days. I had waited my entire life for this moment and had trained extremely hard. I desperately wanted to be drafted.

We watched it all unfold in the two-bedroom apartment I shared with Ka'aina. It was Jill, my mom, Kevin, Colleen, Ka'aina, and me. Jack, my agent, a fiery type who'd been around the league a long time and represented dozens of players, was in touch by phone, and working the angles.

The 2003 draft was seven rounds long, and 262 players got picked. All of them were rated as more valuable than me: I was not one of the 262.

While my family and girlfriend and best friend remained in the living room, I retreated to my bedroom and shut the door. Was this like my grandfather, Howdo, who could be all rambunctious one minute, then retreat to a room to be silent and morose the next? No, of course not. I had every reason to be upset! This was it, the end of my journey—unless I attracted interest as a free agent. As I lay in bed staring out at the pine trees, Jack called to say that it looked as if I might not even get picked up as a free agent. There was a pause on his end—then he asked about my dad. Could he maybe get me into NFL Europe?

I was so furious at his question that I hung up on him and punched a hole in the wall. I never imagined having to use my dad and "connections" to get me into pro football.

Was it a pipe dream all along? Yeah, I guess so.

Or maybe not. Three hours after the 262nd and final NFL draft pick was selected (the Oakland Raiders chose Gustavus Adolphus College wide receiver Ryan Hoag, who never played a down in the NFL), Jack called back to say that the Dallas Cowboys were offering me a $5,000 bonus to attend their rookie mini-camp.

How did that happen? They hadn't even sent a scout to my combine!

Growing up in New Jersey as a fan of the New York Giants, I hated the Cowboys. Now I loved them. Kevin and Ka'aina left our suddenly festive apartment to go to the mall and buy a bunch of Cowboys shirts and hats for everyone. When they got back, Ka'aina told me that Kevin, my hero, who was probably the better athlete between the O'Neil brothers, had cried tears of joy for me. Meanwhile, Mom and Colleen cooked a huge London broil dinner for all of us. Some of my teammates, and Coach Lees, the linebacker coach who had been so supportive, stopped by to celebrate.

But I knew just how tough it would be to make the Dallas Cowboys, also known as America's Team. *Don't get ahead of yourself,* I told myself over and over. This was just for rookie mini-camp, not actual training camp. If they'd really liked me, they would have spent their last pick on me. (Instead, they drafted University of Colorado guard Justin Bates, who would never play in the NFL.)

And who was the Cowboys head coach? NFL legend Bill Parcells, who had won two Super Bowls with the New York Giants and had also cut my father from the New England Patriots the day I was born.

Was that good or bad?

I knew that no one hustled more than I did. I *had* to: I played linebacker in college at 6-foot, 225 pounds, significantly undersized for a linebacker in the NFL. I compensated with speed and instincts, by understanding the quickest way to the point of attack. Almost everyone who knew me as a football player would call me "intense." Coach Lees liked to say I could not be blocked. That I was "slimy"—high football praise.

And if I couldn't make the Cowboys as a starting linebacker, then I'd have to show them that they needed me as a special teams player—that particular beast known, more than anyone else on the field, for doing anything it takes.

Chapter 4

PIPE DREAMS AND NO SLEEP

Rookie mini-camp was a three-day evaluation at Valley Ranch, in Irving, Texas, the Cowboys main practice facility and a 20-minute drive from Dallas. Honestly, rookie camp is really a tryout but no one calls it that. "Camp" sounds less threatening, though if you don't do well, you won't get asked to attend the main camp. It was held in May 2003, two months before the team's full, six-week training camp. I was paid a minimal per diem, plus the five thousand dollars they offered me. There were about two dozen other players there—seven draft picks and the rest of us non-draftees, which included three quarterbacks, and the remainder of the guys split between defense and offense.

My first morning, while walking into the practice complex for the first time, I was daydreaming about when I'd meet the famous head coach and famous owner. As I opened the door to the first long hallway, right there, walking straight at me, were Coach Parcells and owner Jerry Jones.

I completely blanked. I said something I couldn't recall even as I was saying it, and stumbled my way through an awkward exchange.

"Well, it's good to have you here, Keith," Mr. Jones said in conclusion.

"Well, it's good to have you here, too," I replied, as I waved at them and moved on down the hall, immediately feeling like an idiot. *It's good to have you here, too?* He's the owner! Of course he's going to be here!

Sure, I felt anxious: This was *the* opportunity I had been gunning for since I started Pop Warner in eighth grade—and even from further back, when Kevin (on his knees) and I played football in our family room, pillows covering the pointy furniture. Yet despite a dumb, forgivable remark to Mr. Jones, I was able to focus on the tasks before me. My Cowboys jersey, number fifty-four—they picked it—was hanging in my locker. I got dressed deliberately, trying to remember the moment even as I was living it. Then, I went out and ran a 4.58 40-yard dash, fast for a linebacker. I bench-pressed 225 pounds 24 times; weightlifting had always come naturally. I did the other requirements—cone drills, shuttles, etc., and lots of physicals. Throughout every practice I hustled my ass off. (Everyone there is hustling his ass off, so to stand out you have to hustle even harder.) Rookie camp lasted for three days, and I thought I did pretty well.

Would I be part of their future? I flew back to Arizona to finish the last weeks of the school year. Three weeks later, the phone rang. It was the Cowboys. They wanted to discuss my travel arrangements to the main training camp.

That did not mean that I made the team—not by a long-shot. Ninety players are invited to training camp but only 53 make it, and most of those spots are already reserved for stars, other veterans, and the very top draft picks. What it *did* mean was that for the last few years, I had not been living a complete delusion.

I can't tell you why things changed so much. It's a question I have asked myself often in the years since.

Why was I okay at rookie camp, where a bad performance would have sealed my fate just as much as it would at the next level? Was it that, at the full training camp, I was that much closer to realizing my dream?

No, I don't think that's it. But I honestly do not have an answer. I don't know why the undiagnosed mental illness inside me started taking root as I was on the edge of making my lifelong dream a reality.

As if anyone understands who we *really* are.

At the main training camp, in the brutal August heat of San Antonio, all the team's stars and regulars were there: Terence Newman, Darren Woodson, Larry Allen, Dat Nguyen, Flozell Adams, and more. I was a little intimidated by Coach Parcells, one of the greatest, most legendary coaches in the history of the game—even though, like him, I considered myself a "no-nonsense" guy. Punctuality was a religion for him. And he was fair, treating the guy trying to make the

53rd and final roster spot the same way he treated the stars and top draft picks.

From the start, I was concerned that I might have trouble with the playbook. In college, we didn't even bother with one. I was good enough to play off of instinct, so they just let me line up and operate with minimal reins.

But that kind of approach wouldn't cut it in the NFL.

My bigger problem, though, was that the insomnia of my youth had returned like never before. From the start of camp I constantly felt anxious. Even though I was punishing my body at practice during the day, at night my sleep was fitful at best. I hoped it was just first-day jitters—but it continued for nights and days on end. Maybe it came down to this: Trying out for the Dallas Cowboys, trying to make any NFL team, is stressful enough. It's especially so for someone with a mental illness. And maybe even more so for someone who doesn't yet know that he has such an illness.

Drinking to ease the reality was not an option—certainly not if I wanted to perform at an NFL level. I started taking Nyquil and Unisom to help with sleep, but they provided virtually no relief. I got some Ambien from a Cowboys trainer.

At practice, Coach Parcells was often intimidating, even scary. Sometimes we practiced inside the Alamodome. Other times, to get out, we traveled to a local high school to practice, feel the sunshine, the wind, real grass. No matter where we were, though, we always knew where Coach was, even if he was two practice fields or a couple hundred yards away. After the first week, I was pent up and exhausted but also felt as if I had shown a lot on the field. I got the sense that Coach liked what he was seeing from me, and it didn't hurt my chances that he gave such incredible emphasis to special teams. While defensive meetings were attended only by defensive players and coaches, and offensive meetings only by the offense, special teams meetings were attended by everyone on the team. It didn't matter which position you played or coached: You had to be in the special teams meetings.

Our first preseason game was on August 9, 2003. The night before the game—on the road, against the Arizona Cardinals—I again couldn't sleep, which made my current anxiety that much more of a burden. How would it hurt my performance on the field the next day?

Apparently not at all: I played extremely well. I had an interception and was involved in more tackles and stops than I could keep track of. After the game, I moved from fourth on the linebacker depth chart to second.

The game over, my performance a hit, my status climbing, we returned to San Antonio, where I proceeded to go most of the week without sleeping.

~

My anxiety increased dramatically, the pressure got heavier, my mind raced. I lost fifteen pounds in ten days, my weight falling to 219. I was too distraught to eat.

Once each practice session began, the physical exertion and adrenaline brought my mind and body back to high-performance mode. Somehow I always did well when my mind had a specific goal. It was between the two-a-days and then after, when my teammates slept, that I would break down. I had gone through severe injuries as an athlete but never in my life had I experienced such agony. I was approaching my next NFL preseason game on four consecutive sleepless nights and counting.

In my head, I promised anyone who could hear—God, Parcells, Jerry Jones, my parents, Kevin, Colleen, Jill—*anything*, for just a couple hours of sleep.

I'm sure you know that this was unsustainable, and dangerous, for any human being. Sleep deprivation is commonly used as a torture technique because of what it does to you, particularly psychologically.

And maybe I wasn't hiding my fatigue and stress as well as I thought. At one point, in between two-a-days at the Alamodome, I was in the locker room putting on my equipment. My mind hurt, my body hurt. My lips were terribly chapped from nervously licking them all the time, just one of many unpleasant side effects of my being underslept. My eyes burned. My heart was beating out of my chest. I was shaking. My short-term memory was gone. My linebacker coach was suddenly standing in front of me.

"Keith, do you know Jesus?"

I was shocked by the question and not interested to engage—or feeling capable of engaging.

"Yes, I know Jesus," I managed, hoping that would end our awkward encounter.

He looked at me for several more seconds, then walked away.

It wasn't the religious part of the question that troubled me. It was that he saw something that made him approach me, a distraught look that told him that something was wrong. And if he saw it, well . . . were all the coaches talking in meetings about my mental state? Had Coach Parcells noticed? Were they wondering if I was mentally reliable on the field? (I had no doubt that I was physically reliable on the field, and that they knew it.)

Would that be enough to disqualify me from making the team?

I couldn't help but think about how badly I wanted to quit. But I didn't know how. I couldn't quit, not now. I was so close to making the team. I was playing great.

Alone again in the locker room, I put on my cleats.

"Keith."

Coach Parcells, from over my left shoulder, called my name. I quickly turned—and no one was there. I was alone in the locker room.

Quit, and this will all be over, said the voice in my head. *Then you can sleep.*

I called my father's cell. I caught him in the car, with my mother, driving from Buffalo to Pennsylvania to visit family.

"I can't do it anymore," I told my dad. "I'm going to quit." All I wanted, I told him, was to sleep. My mind wouldn't stop. "I don't know what's going on with me."

Dad had pulled the car over to focus completely on what I was telling him. "If that's what you want to do," he finally said, "it's okay with me. If you can wake up in the morning knowing you quit the Cowboys, then it's okay with me, Keith."

Suddenly, Mom was on the phone. She asked how I was doing.

"I'm going to quit."

"You better not. If you quit the Cowboys, you better damn well make sure you can live with that."

I hung up on her, pissed. But whether it was her intention or not, it pushed me just enough in that moment to *not* quit.

Spite and "I'll show you" can work as motivating tools, but they're no replacement for sleep. And I just couldn't. More two-a-days at the Alamodome. I continued—I honestly don't know how—to do well in practice. I simply didn't know how to take a play off. Was I a windup toy on the field?

Was it just pride and the fear of embarrassment? Another practice over, I found myself in the Alamodome, alone. All the lights in the stadium were off and it was completely dark. *I would love to fall asleep right here*, I thought. That's what my teammates, back in their rooms, were all doing at the moment, what you're supposed to do every day between body-depleting practices: sleep.

You know the line from *A League of Their Own*, "There's no crying in baseball!" Well, there's really, *really* no crying in football—at least not in public. Yet there I was, a rookie free agent wannabe ass-kicking linebacker, in the San Antonio Alamodome, preseason practice field of the Dallas Cowboys, America's Team, sitting in the upper stands, as far as possible from the view of owner Jerry Jones or Coach Bill Parcells or other coaches or any teammates, shaking uncontrollably as I talked on the phone to Jill who was back in Flagstaff, tears rolling down my face, trying to explain to her about my anxiety and inability to fall asleep.

You have to be mentally strong to play this game, I was thinking.

Show any ambivalence about what you're doing here, this golden opportunity that so many people wish they had . . . and they'll find someone who won't show doubt.

How could I seek help when players—especially those of us free agents on the fringe doing everything in our power just to make the team—won't even reveal *physical* injuries? The best players are praised not just for how hard they give and take a hit, but for their mental toughness. Was I, with my psychological issues, *really* going to start talking openly about something that was way easier to conceal than a torn Achilles? That could jeopardize my making the team or rising through the ranks? And could I, or any player like me, ever recover from the stigma, the way you can recover from a torn bicep or broken collarbone? Could teammates, coaches, or fans ever look again at a player without remembering, *Oh, yeah, he's the one who was once too nervous or depressed to play.*

Our next preseason game was the following day, August 15, against the Houston Texans. I got some more Ambien from the team trainer, hush hush. I washed down two pills with an entire bottle of Nyquil. Lying in bed, knowing that tomorrow I again had to prove myself, I desperately needed to sleep.

No luck. My body would jolt and I would break into a cold sweat and my prayers for sleep went unanswered. The only "answers" I heard were voices startling me and preventing me from sleep, voices of play calls echoing through my room as if I were still on the practice field. *Down right, down right, bandit bandit.* Was I dreaming? I looked at the clock. *No, you are not dreaming. Only ten minutes have passed since you last looked at it.*

My roommate, Eric Bickerstaff, a rookie running back from the University of Wisconsin, slept like a baby, night after night. He was also an undrafted free agent. I wondered: How did *he* fall asleep so easily? How did he stay asleep like that? I had never envied anyone as much as I did Eric's ability to nod off.

By the time the following day arrived, I was delusional. Still, I continued to fight. My will to make the team was stronger than whatever forces were trying to stop me.

Because of the drugs and fogginess, I was in a different world throughout the game. But, once again, I played great. Fumble recovery, lots of stops and sharp blocks. I was lined up against a special teams veteran and shut him down every play. There was no way that I hadn't solidified my spot on the roster.

I still don't understand how I got through that game, mentally or physically. But I realized how powerful the mind is, how strong the human will, if you truly want something.

That night, again, I didn't sleep, making it five in a row . . . or was it six? The next night, finally, I slept for three hours. My parents and Kevin, back in Buffalo, resolved to remain awake until morning. They told me that they had all made a deal with God that if *they* stayed up the whole night, *I* should be allowed to sleep. So they had lots of coffee going and the TV on, and they played cards all night. Apparently I called them often, and then, finally, the phone went silent for three hours and they rejoiced to think it was because I had actually fallen asleep. I guess I had.

While my sleep eventually returned to something closer to normal, thanks maybe to lots of Ambien, my anxiety did not subside.

During "stretch," our warm-ups before practice, Coach Parcells came over to tell me that he hoped to find a spot for me on the roster. It might have been his way of preparing me to be part of the practice squad—the guys who just miss making the team but are kept around as extra bodies for practice.

The third preseason game, on August 21 against the Pittsburgh Steelers, I again played well.

On the following Thursday night against the Oakland Raiders, our final preseason game, I blindsided the Raiders cover guy on a kickoff return, knocking him out cold and freeing our return guy to go all the way for a touchdown. I also had a sack at a crucial part of the game. Would I get a star on my helmet? (Rookies don't get to have a star on their helmet until they make the team.)

Preseason was done. The next big moment would be in two to three days, Saturday or Sunday, when the team would make their final cuts. I tried to block out everything else, hoping I wouldn't be one of those who gets a visit from "The Turk"— the name everyone in the league uses for the guy on each team who waits for you, like the Grim Reaper, to lead you to a room where they let you go, ending your career with the team and often with football forever, with those horrible words no player ever wants to hear: "And we'll need your playbook."

The day after the Oakland game, with the team gathered to watch film, Coach Parcells started with the kickoff return touchdown.

"This kid, number fifty-four, is going to make this team," Parcells said in the dark room to the entire team. "We need more number fifty-fours."

That day, before final cuts were announced and unbeknownst to me, Coach Parcells called my father. Maybe he did it that way because my father was an old football man himself, or because Coach had cut my dad from the Pats twenty-three years earlier, ending his playing career. Maybe Coach just had a special feeling for my kind of player, a grunt who did everything asked of him and more.

"Ed," said Coach, "I called to tell you that you and your wife raised a hell of a boy. And he's going to make our football team."

"Talking with Keith on the phone last week, he told me that during stretch you said you were going to try to find a spot for him," my father replied. "So does this mean he'll be on the practice squad?"

"No, he's on the varsity," said Coach. "He'll be playing in the opener next week against Atlanta."

My father was at a loss for words.

"But you're not allowed to tell Keith because cuts aren't until Sunday."

"We talk to Keith several times a day," my father said, "so how do we not tell him?"

"Well, just don't."

My father thanked him. True to his word, he and Mom said nothing to me in our regular phone calls for the next two days.

On Saturday, while I was working out in the weight room, Coach Parcells came by to tell me that I had made the team, one of four non-draftees to accomplish that feat.

Yep, it was official. No pipe dream.

~

About 1 in 15 high school football players play at the varsity college level. Of those college players about 1 in 60 play in the NFL. And almost all of those who make an NFL team are drafted by the league. Maybe 50 guys each year make a team without being drafted.

It wasn't just that the odds were stacked against me. Much as my family and friends and coaches cared for me, I was pretty sure that none of them expected me to do what I did. From my mediocre grades to my attending a Division I-AA school to my being not *that* big to my getting only so-so playing time my first two years in college to my getting passed over as a junior, only to have fate step in . . . forget my "pedigree" as the son of a former NFL linebacker. There were a bunch of reasons it was a long shot that "the League" would be my first job out of college. I couldn't blame anyone for not really believing I'd make it.

The first week of the regular season, I signed for the rookie league minimum of $225,000.

My parents would tell me, much later, that they thought once training was over and I had made the team, the worst was behind us.

But it was difficult for me to enjoy the moment. You would think I would be ecstatic. More than anything, though, I was relieved. Thoughts of the regular season, which started in seven days, filled my mind. As I prepared for the Falcons, I realized I would once again have to deal with the two-headed monster of anxiety and insomnia.

I did treat myself to one present: a GMC Yukon. It was unlike me. I was always conservative with money, and didn't really need the truck.

Later in the week, when Coach Parcells was doing a press conference to talk about the team's prospects and upcoming season, he referred to me. "He is scrappy and he's going to be dangerous," he said. "I mean dangerous," he repeated.

Neither of us knew then just how true the last part of that description was.

Chapter 5

SCRAPPY AND DANGEROUS

Rudy . . . Rudy . . .

More than one local newspaper article compared me to "Rudy"—the undersized, not particularly talented, steel-willed Rudy Ruettiger of University of Notre Dame football lore whose story was the basis for the inspirational movie, *Rudy*, which is in endless rotation on cable TV. The kind of guy about whom you might say, "You can't measure heart with a stopwatch."

I was a much better football player than Rudy but, in a way, even less likely to have made the team I tried out for. Outwardly, I was making my mark. I was fast and hit with authority. I was determined, even a bit wild. Inwardly, I was incredibly anxious. Coach Parcells didn't know that about me yet—at least, I didn't *think* he did: When my linebacker coach asked me about Jesus, it freaked me out to think that all the coaches, and maybe my teammates, could see what a fragile, nervous mess I was. But that was probably me being paranoid, another trait of the sleep-deprived. Aside from Jill and my immediate family and very closest friends, no one knew about my situation. I hid it well (or tried to, at least). The only time I truly expressed my anxiety in a public way was productively, on the football field, especially for the three hours during games. The intensity and unpredictability and strict rules and hard boundaries of a football game were the perfect way for me to unleash whatever was going on inside my head. You know what's expected of you, so you do it. Underneath the uniform, the shoulder pads, the helmet was someone who had very little control over what was happening in his mind or with his emotions, but could use his body in a way that made all the rest an afterthought.

As far as everyone else was concerned, I was a success story. A guy who got along. An inspiration.

Rudy.

During a day off, while I sat in the Cowboys steam room, a scout walked by. "O'Neil, thank you!" he shouted. "You made me ten thousand bucks!"

"How'd I do that?"

"Coach Parcells said if an undrafted free agent makes the team, the scout that brought him in gets a ten thousand dollar bonus."

"But how did you find me?" I asked. Northern Arizona was not a hotbed of football. I didn't recognize him from the pro day I put on for myself.

"Remember your junior year," he said, "when you guys were playing Sam Houston State in the playoffs and you chased that receiver down on a reverse and caught him from twenty yards behind?"

I did. It was the kind of highlight play you remember, if you happen to be involved. "Yeah, I remember."

"*That's* why you're a Dallas Cowboy. That one play. And you know what? I wasn't even there to watch you. I was scouting a player on Sam Houston." He smiled. He was a small man, very old, with the whitest hair, and he had no doubt seen a lot. "You never know who's watching."

And now I was actually here. I grew up believing that things happen for a reason, and I eventually told myself that maybe if I *had* attended a bigger, "better" school like my brother had, I *wouldn't* have made the NFL. Kevin was a phenomenal high school athlete, starring in football and track. He was 6-foot-3, 195 pounds, and could run like hell. He got to Syracuse, which was loaded with talent, and they red-shirted him freshman year. He had gone to college as a wide receiver but they moved him to safety for a year or two. He wasn't a safety. So they moved him to linebacker. The two guys in front of him both went on to the NFL, so he didn't see much playing time. I wondered if the same thing would have happened to me if I had played at a big school.

Even at NAU, what if the junior college transfer brought in to start ahead of me had not broken his leg the third play of the season? As much as it takes talent to make the NFL, it also requires timing and opportunity—not a little luck. Yet I was also proud to think that by making it to the NFL, I had beat out players from Division I-A schools like Notre Dame, USC, Tennessee, Virginia Tech, LSU, Minnesota, Akron, etc. And if *that* was true, then I *could* have started at any of those schools. Who said I had a chip on my shoulder? When I was with the Cowboys and later the Colts, I always looked to see the alma maters of the players I was competing against for a roster spot.

Now I was #54 on the Dallas Cowboys. The same number that Cowboy legends Chuck Howley and Randy White had worn.

We had a good team in 2003, not dominant, but strong enough to challenge for a playoff spot. Halfway through my rookie season, Coach Parcells approached me one day as I walked in from practice.

"O'Neil, you're doing a great job," he said. "You're on your way to being a great special teamer. You can run and you can hit." My teammates had started to call me "Salty" because of the way I carried myself, a little bit pissed-off or even mean, my expression like I was reacting to a salty taste in my mouth. I kind of liked it.

During the season I lived at TownePlace Suites, where rookies stayed during mini and training camp. I was the only one of the 53 Cowboy players who never left. I just didn't need the distraction of finding a new place. I made friends with several teammates, including our All-Pro tight end and future Hall of Famer Jason Witten, one of the most down-to-earth people you could ever meet. But I didn't need much company. I was fine being on my own.

I had also become addicted to Ambien. My tolerance grew during the season. I learned how the drug worked. I realized that, for me, after taking it I had about a twenty-minute window to fall asleep, after which the drug's power would wear off. I could feel it wanting to work and I would find a way to talk myself out of sleep, which was why I needed at least three pills to have a chance. Eventually, I would hallucinate myself to sleep: I would be trying to fall asleep and start imagining I was watching myself sleep, but I'd still be awake and part of me knew I was still awake. It was sort of like a waking dream.

None of this, however, stopped me from playing well. I finished the season second on the team in special team tackles. I had only one play at linebacker all season, during a goal-line stand against the New England Patriots in Foxboro on November 16. But I felt confident that I had established my value to the team.

During my first offseason with the Cowboys (I lived in Irving; lots of the team also lived in the Dallas area, making it easy to work out at the facilities), Jason Witten, his wife Michelle, an old college friend of Jason's, and I all decided to go out on the town. It was St. Patrick's Day and my name is O'Neil, so it's a bit of a given. Jason and Michelle stayed relatively sober, but Jason's friend and I had too much.

At one point we took a limousine to an area in Dallas called Greenville that's overflowing with bars. Not that it mattered how many bars there were, because by the time we stepped out of the limo I was already severely intoxicated. The night was blurry. Before I knew what was going on, I was fighting with a bouncer who wouldn't let me in the bar because I was too drunk.

My next memory was of the back of a paddy wagon.

The following morning, I found myself lying on a ratty foam pad on the floor of a jail cell. They gave me back my belt and shoelaces and released me. I was charged with public intoxication, a Class C misdemeanor. I had to pay a small fine and that would be it.

Of course, that was *not* it. Walking out of jail, I had only a vague idea of where I was and even less of what I was going to do. I could not remember what had happened the night before or what I did. It was *The Hangover* without the laughs.

One thing I knew for certain was that I was probably in big trouble.

As my eyes adjusted to the bright Texas sun, I saw Jason sitting in his truck, waiting for me. Jason was a standup guy; he always knew the right thing to do. The night before, he and his wife just wanted to have a good time and I had to ruin it with my out-of-control drinking. On the ride back to my apartment, we discussed what I should do. Tell Coach? Would the media find out? Would I get fined? Kicked off the team?

Back at my place, alone, I was extremely hung over and, of course, very scared. Sometimes you don't do the right thing but you still know the right thing to do. In this case, I just didn't know the right thing to do. After hours of contemplating and back-and-forth phone calls with Jason and Jill, I finally understood that I had to call the Cowboys director of player development. His job was to "be there" for the players—help them, encourage them, troubleshoot, be there in times of need. I called him, told him the basics, and we agreed that I needed to tell Coach Parcells.

This was going to be fun.

Luckily for me, I was still extremely hung over when I got to Coach's office. My altered state helped to block the anxiety, the nerves. I walked straight into his office and proceeded to tell him the whole, ugly truth.

"Coach," I said (I think), "I was out last night, had too much to drink, blacked out, and was thrown in the drunk tank for the night."

He barely looked at me. After what seemed like a very long pause, he said, "I told you guys not to go out, not to go to the clubs. Anything you do past midnight, you're asking for trouble." He shook his head. "Get out of my office."

That was it.

I walked quickly to get outside, climbed into my truck, and drove home. For now, it seemed, the incident was over—but what would happen next?

Several weeks later, I was in the weight room. Coach Parcells had not spoken to me since I had told him about my arrest. Now, while I was lifting, out of nowhere he was standing over me.

"Hey, Greenville," he said. "You gonna put more weight on that bar or what?"

Greenville was the neighborhood with all the bars.

And that was Coach's new nickname for me, at least for a while. Greenville. He used it on me in the weight room and on the practice field. He made his point. And I had it coming.

Later in the offseason, I found a FedEx envelope from the NFL sitting in my locker. The letter stated that I had been fined $11,000 for "misconduct"—my drunken night in Greenville. (I would later learn that the nickname for a fine from the league was "Fedex," because that's how it shows up.) I never found out how the league came up with the figure of $11,000. It was without a doubt the largest bar tab I ever had to pay.

Starting in late May, I was part of OTAs—"organized team activities," which are off-season, non-mandatory practices, meetings, and conditioning workouts. Veterans attend, as well as players recently drafted out of college and undrafted free agents. Some players come for part of it, some not at all.

On the first day there, my insomnia returned, with a ven-
geance. I did not sleep the first night, then the second, then
the third.

On the fourth day of absolutely no sleep, I found Coach
Parcells in the hallway next to the locker room and handed
him my playbook.

"I quit," I told him.

Chapter 6

BEAT THE DEMON

As I offered my playbook to Coach Parcells, I was okay with what I was doing—or as "okay" as a horribly sleep-deprived human being thinks he is. I felt I had proven myself. I had made the NFL. I had shown I could play in it, and did so for an entire season. Unlike most players, *I* would cut the ties. I wasn't being kicked to the gutter. I had no reservations about quitting.

Come on, who was I kidding? That wasn't why I was pushing my playbook at Coach Parcells. I was doing it because I didn't know how to ask for help, though I desperately needed it. So I tried to convince myself I was a success at football, therefore I could move on.

Coach looked at me hard.

"*What*? Are you crazy?"

"I haven't slept in three days," I told him simply. "I don't know what's going on."

Coach was tough. Everyone knew that. Like almost every coach I had ever known, including my father, he lived for the game. He was hard not only on his players but extremely hard on his coaches, too, which made it a tough atmosphere to work in: Even the coaches were walking around with tight asses. For Coach, football came before everything.

But now, a genuinely kind look came over his face. He refused to take my playbook and instead led me to his office. It was hard for me to focus on anything he said because of my sleep deprivation, but I didn't forget the gist.

"Everyone has a demon in their head," he said. His eye contact was intense. It felt so different from the last time I was in his office and had told him I'd been arrested for drunkenness. "And we have to beat that demon. Beat the demon!"

He gave me time to let his message sink in. Before I knew it, we were discussing the playbook. I told him I was having a hard time keeping up. Again, the look he gave me was kind—not quite a smile but full of empathy and encouragement. He told me that I was doing a hell of a job. He told me to keep it up.

It was a side to Coach Parcells I had not seen before and, to be honest, did not know existed. Not that I thought he was a bad guy. I just had not seen this genuinely caring part of him before.

I felt better. I walked out clutching my playbook.

But again: Who was I kidding? His brief pep talk, no matter how warm and inspiring, could not possibly be all that was needed.

I practiced that day. That night, I lay awake until sunrise.

I still wanted it just to be over—the stress, the pressure, the anxiety. I just wanted to sleep peacefully. There was nothing specific I had in mind that would make me happier than playing in the NFL. I had no other dreams. But I was pretty sure I could get a decent job with the NFL on my résumé.

And that just showed how far gone I was. I actually got it in my head that the "real world" would be easier for someone like me.

I never *really* asked for help until I knew that I absolutely, positively needed it. In college and before, I did not understand that how I behaved or what I felt was a bigger problem than I assumed it was. I didn't think it was much different from what many people, maybe most people, think and go through. It was in my head. It was inside me. If others experienced the same thing, wouldn't it also be tucked away for them like it was for me?

Especially if you're a guy. Especially if you're 6-foot, 240 pounds, and can run down wide receivers from behind, bench-press 225 pounds 24 times, and know how to handle yourself in a fistfight. Especially if you're a player in the National Football League.

At times, I knew something was up with me mentally. (And I wasn't including getting arrested for being too drunk, fighting, or locking myself in a bathroom to light candles and pray for sleep.) I never got to the root of it, though, because *I did not know how.* At least in my family, we didn't talk about mental issues. No one talked about my grandfather's "problem." And I'm not blaming my family, not at all. I'm not sure how families with one or more members who suffer from mental illness talk about it. Especially before it gets diagnosed. And at this point, I had a long, long way to go before I would be diagnosed.

And it's not just the individuals who don't talk about it, or the families of those people. It's everyone. Society very rarely talks about mental issues in a meaningful way. I wasn't taught about it in school. I certainly wasn't taught about it in church. (In a way, Coach Parcells' "Beat the demon!" pep talk sounded like something a priest or minister would say, without much interest in how the demon got in there to begin with or whether the demon could be beaten or at least managed better with proper medication.) So how would I know how to speak to someone about it? How would my family? How would a linebacker ever know what to do in a Cover 2 defense unless he had been specifically trained do it?

Years later, after I "went public" with what I had (or what I was) and understood myself and my condition a little better, it disappointed me that so many people still couldn't or wouldn't talk about it. If they had seen that I had a broken leg, you could be sure they would ask how I was doing. Even if I had cancer, which not everyone is comfortable talking about because of the serious nature of the sickness, lots of people would still ask about the chemo or how my energy was or maybe how I was holding up emotionally.

When people know you have a mental illness? Sometimes, crickets.

It wasn't until later that I could appreciate the meaning of my attempt to hand my playbook to Coach Parcells and quit football. Because as I prepared for my second training camp with the Cowboys, the focus and release of the game helped a little bit to mask the fact that my problem went beyond football. Drinking had helped me to mask things, too, but I couldn't drink in the NFL. My moment with Parcells was a cry for help, and neither of us fully appreciated it.

My second training camp, in the summer of 2004, was held in Oxnard, California. I'm not sure why they moved there from San Antonio but the practice fields, facilities, hotel, and especially the weather were all better than they had been in Texas. I roomed with Jason; both of us were entering our second year in the league. I was taking Ambien nightly but my insomnia wasn't plaguing me the way it had at OTAs or at training camp the year before. Even my anxiety was a notch down from what it had been my rookie year. Still, at my level—special teamer, backup linebacker, undrafted, league minimum salary—there was no guarantee of making the team again. I improved my special teams technique with help from Bruce DeHaven, one of the all-time great special teams coaches. He taught me a move he called "scraping paint" that enabled me to keep from blocking in the back, a frequent penalty on punt and kickoff returns.

I played well during preseason and kept my spot on the team. Coach Parcells believed that your rookie year you get "the benefit of the doubt," but you had better show real development the following year to make the team again. I suppose I cleared that bar. Getting hammered in Greenville and being thrown in the drunk tank, along with trying to quit the team, apparently did not affect my ability to perform on the field.

The season was less of a struggle than training camp. Maybe the security that came with it, along with the renewed pride and sense of accomplishment, had something to do with that. (*Maybe.*) I still had a full-on addiction to Ambien, and it didn't even always work because of the tolerance I'd built up.

As with so many athletes, the games were my release. Once I stepped on the field, my heart was going 120 miles per hour. My body was ready to hit someone. I just wanted the first hit to be over. Soon as that happened, the game seemed to take care of itself.

On Tuesdays, our day off, players often went to the Cowboys complex in the morning to get some rehab, maybe get in a quick lift (I hated weightlifting and did it only when I had to), or sit in the cold tubs or hot tubs, depending on how you felt. The afternoons were for golf (my game was terrible), sitting home with family, or doing your own thing if you didn't have family around. For the first time that year, I got to play on the beautiful Cowboys-only golf course. Coach Parcells, a single-digit handicap golfer, saw I was clueless and gave me some tips. One time I brought Jill to the course, where Coach got to meet her for the first time. He was totally charmed. He looked at her, then me, then her, then me.

"O'Neil," he said, shaking his head, "you outkicked your coverage."

Going out to dinner with teammates could be fun. But because I tended to be a loner, I often dined out by myself, especially those first two years when Jill was still in school and only able to visit me on occasion. I didn't mind being alone, though having Jill there was of course better. When she was around, she and I, Jason and Michelle Witten, and Tony Romo and his girlfriend at the time went out to dinner a lot.

Home games were more relaxing than away games, especially now that I had my own place, a modest house close to the Cowboys complex. When playing at home, you of course had more time with family and friends, though the night before the game you still had to go to the Airport Marriott where we all had meals, meetings, and curfew.

Traveling for road games was fun. It was cool to visit cities and play in other stadiums. My second favorite was Lambeau Field in Green Bay, the Packers' home field. It wasn't just the history embedded in the place but the fact that it was bowl-shaped, not tiered, like most NFL stadiums. In a bowl it feels much more like a college stadium. But my favorite place to play was Giants Stadium, because of my history there when I was a kid and its proximity to my childhood home. Once, I got to play in a Monday night game, representing the Cowboys against the hated (though not to me) rival New York Giants. The edge of New York City, at night, with the sports world watching. It truly felt electric, as if for one night I was at the center of the universe.

Whatever city we were in, we would get a group of guys to go out for dinner. Wherever we went, crowds of people lined up for autographs and photos. Being an NFL player, especially on the Dallas Cowboys, was a little different from being a football star at Sweet Home High School in Amherst, New York, or a Northern Arizona University Lumberjack.

As celebrated as we were, we were not very good: We followed up my rookie season, where we were 10–6 and lost in a wildcard playoff game, to 6–10.

After the 2004 season, Jill came to Texas to live with me. She got a job as a nurse at the Children's Hospital of Dallas. We got engaged and planned a Dallas wedding for the following year.

At my third training camp, I learned something that was not in my control, and which created a new obstacle: During the offseason, the team decided to switch from a 4-3 defense, where you have three linebackers, so they each need to be faster, to a 3-4 defense, where you have four linebackers, so they each need to be bigger.

Not great news for a linebacker who was more fast than big. My value to the team now hinged almost totally on my special teams ability. As good as I was there, and as much as Coach Parcells cared about special teams play, I didn't know if it would be enough.

In practice, I never took off a play, meaning giving less than 100 percent. If you're a veteran or a high-round draft pick, now and then you'll take plays off in practice. (You never take plays off in a game.) I didn't care if other players took a play off. I only cared about myself. Me, I went 110 percent on every snap, every practice.

It was my best pro training camp yet. Guys I respected, stellar defensive players like Dat Ngyuen and Terence Newman, told me how much I'd improved on defense.

My addiction to Ambien eased, but I still had trouble sleeping. And I was still having a hard time with the playbook. Not that my mind couldn't grasp it: I knew it backward and forward . . . until I stepped on the field, when I would start to forget some things. Was it anxiety? Years later, I would learn that anxiety and also hypomania, a common symptom of bipolar I disorder, can both affect memory.

And maybe going 110 percent on every play had its downside. Maybe I was training *too* hard. Coach started calling me out for being "reckless" in practice. I could see him getting pissed because I knew only one speed. I did not realize it then, but I later understood that he was trying to tell me that I did not know how to practice like a veteran, and I probably needed to learn, fast.

Once, in between two-a-days in the weight room, while lifting and minding my own business, I was approached by my linebacker coach, the same one who had asked me a couple years before if I knew Jesus.

Something was up. He rarely entered the weight room.

"Keith, do you have a learning disability?" he asked.

My heart fell. I was surprised by the question, and also humiliated: Teammates were within earshot.

"No," I said.

He walked away.

That's it? *That's* what he wanted to ask me?

It was the first time in my life that anyone had questioned my intelligence—and suddenly it was the first time that I questioned it, too. Hadn't my college coach called me a "real fast learner"?

First, I had to get past what a supremely jerky move it was for the coach to do what he did, like that. If he sensed I was struggling, if he needed to ask me that question, couldn't he at least have brought me into his office?

Fact is, I knew my playbook; I probably studied it *too* much. I obsessed over it. But when I got on the field, I struggled. I don't know why. Some of it was the different terminology between zone coverage and man coverage, between blitzes and zone pressures. You had to know what everyone on your defense was doing *and* recognize what the offense was doing. The anxiety, the fatigue, the millions of thoughts flying through my head didn't help—let alone the pressure. Before I got in the league I had barely ever opened a playbook in my life because I didn't have to. We didn't even have one in high school or college. I knew what I had to do and where I had to go. Most of the time I could sense what the opposing offense was going to do before they did it.

But now the coach had me wondering: *Could I have a learning disability? Was I intellectually or mentally limited in some areas?* When I had to make quick decisions under pressure, when the cameras were rolling and everyone was watching, I struggled—on defense, that is, where it takes at least a split-second of deliberation and assessment, never on special teams, which is pretty much pure instinct. Except for a quarterback kneel down at the end of a game or a 100-per-cent-certain passing play when it's third down and very long, special team plays are the only ones where everyone pretty much knows what's going to happen, and it's just a matter of seeing who can go harder at what they do to win the battle.

The coach wasn't questioning my instinct, however, but my mind. What was I supposed to do about that?

I didn't have time to let the comment fully sink in, when he passed me again and asked, sincerely this time and with-out others around, how I was doing and if I was okay. He must have sensed something was wrong.

I lied that I was fine. Later, I thought of a few things I'd wished I'd said to him, including that right then, while play-ing in the NFL, I was also completing my last three credits to earn my degree from NAU. How many guys on the team were doing that? True, I was about to get a liberal studies degree without once ever opening a book, and I don't say that with pride. (At the end of each semester, I would return my books to the campus bookstore with the plastic wrapping still on them.) But I don't care who you ask: You have to be smart to graduate from college without reading one page, right?

One day at practice, about a week before final cuts, Coach Parcells approached me. "Have you ever played full-back before?"

"Yes, a little," I said. "When I was a freshman in college. And in high school, a lot."

He surveyed me up and down, like he hadn't looked at me before. Actually, my body was more classic fullback than classic linebacker.

"Be ready," he said. "We might need you there." If it sounds as if that was maybe a good thing: It wasn't. I knew it was probably a bad thing. As he walked away, I wondered just how numbered were my days as a Cowboy. Asking me if I played fullback was his way of saying without saying that they were looking for other positions that I might play. Meaning they had pretty much given up on me at linebacker.

The thought of getting cut began to sink in.

For the last several days of preseason, each time I walked out of the complex through the doors that led to the parking lot, I walked with my head down, scared that The Turk would be standing right beyond the last set of doors, waiting.

When the last practice before final cuts was done, I once again made my way down the hall, this time talking with Brett Pierce, a tight end. We were both "on the bubble," nervous about getting cut, wondering if one or both of us would get the ax. I can't remember if I walked faster or slower than usual. As we came to the last set of doors, I looked up.

The Turk.

Please don't make eye contact with me.

"Keith."

He motioned me toward an office door just inside the complex. "Please go into that room."

Brett gave me the most sympathetic look he could in that situation, knowing it just as well could have been him.

I entered the room. The director of player personnel looked up and said, "Keith, I'm sorry to be the bearer of bad news but we have to let you go. Can I please have your playbook?"

Stunned, I just said . . . "Thanks."

They had me sign some papers acknowledging that I was not injured. Then I went to clean out my locker. I couldn't bear to seek out my teammates—guys like Dat Nguyen, from whom I'd learned so much, and Jason, a great player and an even better pal and person. I was getting choked up and didn't want to shed a tear. There is no crying in football.

I was supposed to take only the stuff that I "owned" but I didn't care. I took my helmet, which wasn't technically mine. I took all of my team-issued sweats and clothing, all my cleats and workout shoes, gloves, shampoo, deodorant— everything. The only thing I didn't take were my shoulder pads, which had fit me perfectly. And I left my thigh and knee pads, too. If it wasn't nailed down, though, I took it. Sort of me getting the last laugh.

I threw the stuff into my truck and climbed in. I was emotional, and part of me was startled that I was so emotional when just a year before I was ready to quit so that I could feel some peace. But of course I was emotional! It's a totally different feeling getting cut than quitting.

I called my agent. Jack told me to be patient. He was confident I would get picked up by another team. I drove back to the house Jill and I shared. I walked in and sat down on the couch, completely lost.

I actually said out loud, like something from a bad TV show, "What am I going to do now?"

My mind raced. I became anxious. I jumped back in my truck and drove to the Children's Hospital. I asked the woman at the desk if she would get Jill for me. When Jill came through the double doors, she was already crying: She knew why I was there, in the middle of the day. (When you play in the NFL and you're not a big star, it's not just you who worries about The Turk. Everyone who cares about you worries.) Jill wasn't crying so much because I would no longer be a Cowboy but because we were planning a wedding in Dallas and it was now almost certain that we would be gone from there. If we were lucky, we would *have* to move. Jill would have to find another nursing job.

I told her that Jack felt good that I'd get picked up by another team. I didn't know if he was just being encouraging in a down moment or if he genuinely felt that the type of player I was would get picked up. Either way, he instructed me to just be patient and think positive thoughts.

Chapter 7

NEW BEGINNINGS AND THE TRUE END

Jill and I were lying in bed the next morning, thinking positive thoughts, talking about when the phone would ring . . . when the phone rang.

Area code 317. Indianapolis area. I knew that from when my brother-in-law Drew had played for the Colts.

"Hello?" I answered.

Chris Polian, vice president of football operations for the Indianapolis Colts, introduced himself in a very friendly manner. Then he said, "I have good news, Keith. We just picked you up off waivers and want you to come play special teams for us." The Anti-Turk.

"Thank you, thank you!" I said. "I can do that!"

"We need you to get on a plane as soon as possible because we play the Ravens this weekend," he said, then gave me a contact in the Colts organization to schedule the flight. Again I thanked him, and that was that. I was about to become a member of the Indianapolis Colts, a powerhouse in the AFC South whose talent level was far superior to the Cowboys' at that time, good enough to make a deep playoff run. It was great news all around.

But you can't run from who you are.

Even though it was a new team, new coach, new style, new teammates, new city, new start: The anxiety and sleepless nights, and more, were all set to visit me again. They were not exclusively caused by the Dallas Cowboys.

The equipment glitch didn't help.

I flew to Indianapolis on Monday night, in September of 2005, and began practicing the next morning. Throughout my football-playing life, from Pop Warner to middle school to high school to college to the NFL, I was always OCD about my equipment. It had to fit just right. I liked everything really tight and snug. When it was just so, I felt as if I could hit without distraction. But at Indy, none of the equipment fit the way I liked it. My helmet was loose, my pads bulky and loose. It drove me nuts. The first couple of days of practice the equipment problem gnawed at me. I asked the equipment managers about getting snugger shoulder pads but they seemed uninterested in my problem, busy with a million other things. I took matters into my own hands and called the Cowboys, asking if they would overnight me my shoulder pads. They did, problem solved. (Thankfully, no one in Dallas brought up that I had taken lots of things that didn't belong to me.) The Colts' equipment crew shrugged at the fact that I had swapped out their pads for Cowboy pads.

Was it something as simple and solvable as ill-fitting equipment that could set me off, keeping me up at night and arousing my anxiety by day? Or was it the change in routine? One day I'm wearing a Cowboys helmet in Texas, practically the next I'm wearing a Colts helmet in Indiana. One day I'm following the great and brilliant Parcells' strict routine. Now, I had another great and brilliant coach in Tony Dungy, only he was Parcells' complete opposite: laid-back as it gets.

I felt extreme pressure being a new player on a new team, imagining and then blowing out of proportion what was expected of me. I did not want to let my family and friends down in my new situation. (Not that any of them felt I was a disappointment for getting cut from the Cowboys or would have felt personally let down had I been cut from the Colts—but that's what I *felt*.) Of course, I didn't want to let down my new teammates and coaching staff. Of all the NFL players who got cut right at the end of preseason, of all those suddenly available—and there were hundreds—the Colts had picked my name. During that first week, the linebacker coach approached me in the cafeteria and said, "We think you're going to stick around for a while." How can you not love that? I was eager to repay their belief in me, eager to prove myself again.

Whatever the source of my problem, the same issues arose. Anxiety. Insomnia. And now, increasingly, thoughts of suicide.

Several days of it, in fact. I believed I would never act on the suicidal thoughts, but they were ever-present. I just wanted the whole situation to end—the latest bout of

anxiety and sleeplessness. My thought process went something like this:

I want this to end so bad I want to die,
the only way to die is to commit suicide,
but I won't kill myself, I can't, I don't want to die really,
I want this over, I want to quit.

On and on it went. But though I was thinking about it
every waking moment, I kept it to myself.

On the morning of Saturday, September 10, 2005, the
team was scheduled to fly to Baltimore for the following
day's game against the Ravens. Jill was still asleep in our hotel
room while I—after a sleepless night—stared out the window, thinking about how to "end" this feeling yet not knowing how. Again, given my extreme anxiety and incredible lack
of sleep, my mental state was not to be trusted. I was pretty
sure there was a difference between having suicidal thoughts
and being suicidal, just like there was a difference, someone
would tell me years later, between *having* bipolar and *being*
bipolar. Like there was some bridge you had to cross, and it
was a long tricky bridge. You don't just somehow find yourself on the other end of the bridge, especially when you had
been looking at it from a safe distance for ages.

So there was a difference between *having* suicidal thoughts
and *being* suicidal, right?

Once Jill woke, she and I sat in the living room of our
hotel and I told her I was either going to quit the NFL for
good or get help. I decided to go to the Colts complex early,
still hours before we had to get on the plane, and well before
any other players would be there. I wanted to talk to Coach
Dungy about my issues—but that was as far as my "plan"
went. Jill, seeing how agitated I was to get to the complex
as soon as possible, didn't even bother changing out of her

pajamas. We both threw on coats and shoes and she drove me the ten minutes to the Colts complex, then waited in the car while I went inside.

I walked into the completely empty cafeteria, sat down, and tried to collect my thoughts. I was tired, I was wired—but I also felt a sense of peace. I knew it was all going to be over soon. After ten minutes of thinking and pacing, I pulled out my cellphone and called Coach Dungy. No hesitation, no consideration for what I was doing, none. A guy who had been a Colt for all of five days calling the head coach the morning we were headed out of town to play our first game of the season, a season of sky-high expectations, maybe even a trip to the Super Bowl. To discuss what? A personal issue?

Seriously, what would I say when he picked up?

It went to voicemail. I did not leave a message. I walked to his office, feeling an eerie sense of calm. Sure, maybe I had been with the team for only a few days but I also had the immediate sense from Coach Dungy that I could approach him—even with something like this.

His office was locked. I sat on the floor outside his door and waited.

After maybe fifteen minutes, Dungy showed up.

"Hey, Coach," I said casually enough, though I had no idea what my next words would be. After a breath, I said, "I need to talk to you."

He invited me into his office. As soon as I sat down, I began. "First, I haven't slept in four nights. I'm very anxious. I have a lot of anxiety. I've been dealing with anxiety and sleep problems my whole life. I don't think I can get on the plane today to go to Baltimore to play the Ravens." As I said it, I realized that I didn't want to quit the game or the league, that I never wanted to quit. I just wanted help.

Coach Dungy nodded, taking it in. There was nothing rushed about him. "Okay, I understand, it's okay. We'll get you some help. I just want you to be okay. Are you married?"

Engaged, I told him.

"Does your fiancée know you're here?"

"She's waiting in the car outside. But she's in her pajamas."

Dungy smiled. "That's okay. Bring her in and meet me in the conference room."

I got Jill and we went to the conference room, where we waited for what seemed like an hour.

Finally, Coach Dungy entered along with several other men, who were introduced: Bill Polian, the Colts General Manager and Team President (and future NFL Hall of Fame executive), the head trainer, the team doctor, and my position coach. They were all business. They all looked concerned.

As Coach Dungy led a meeting that he had no idea just an hour before he would be leading, he was just as impressive as Coach Parcells but with a completely different style. Like Coach Parcells, he was understanding.

Coach Dungy asked me to explain to the others what was going on. As I did, part of me was looking down from above on what was happening, with me, a stranger, at the center of it. Here I was, a grown man, twenty-five years old, an NFL special teamer and once-in-a-while linebacker, telling a future Hall of Fame head coach and a future Hall of Fame GM that I could not play in an NFL game because of my anxieties. Because of *stress*. Everyone has stress! But damn it, didn't other people feel this way? Was I such a freak?

You know what? At that moment, I didn't care about any potential embarrassment, fallout, ding to my reputation. I would feel it later, sure, just not right at that moment. I was too in my own head to think of anything but how I felt. (And wasn't that a sign of mental health? Of self-preservation?)

I told the five men seated around the conference table that I could not sleep and that my mind would not stop racing.

I didn't dare mention my suicidal thoughts. I didn't know how.

"Keith, don't worry about it," said Mr. Polian. "We'll get you taken care of. Talk to the doctor. We'll get you back on the field as soon as you're ready."

"You don't have to travel, Keith," said Coach Dungy. "It's okay. Let's just get you back healthy and doing better."

The team doctor said he could prescribe Klonopin, a medicine I would take daily to help with my anxiety. He said he could call it in to my pharmacy. I told him I didn't have a pharmacy because I had just arrived. Jill and I were still living at the Marriott. "Will people find out why I missed the game?" I asked them, suddenly overcome with a sense of what I was doing. Shame was never far. "Media, teammates?"

"No," said Coach Dungy.

"No," said Mr. Polian.

The team trainer spoke up. "Keith, you're not the first one to go through something like this. We have players who have had similar situations."

"And it's okay if I don't play this week?"

"Yes," they all said, almost as one.

I was hopeful about the medication, though surprised the doctor hadn't asked me any deeper questions—you know, my history as a child, as a teen, now as a young man, changes I might have undergone, anything like that. Then again, there were several people in the room, busy people getting ready to fly out of town for the first game of the season. They had taken time from their game preparations to gather in that room and support me, but it probably wasn't an appropriate setting for getting too deep into things.

I asked if I could see someone to talk to, a therapist. The doctor said he would help me get in to see someone within a few days.

Jill and I left the complex. I could not believe it. I was relieved and excited that I was finally getting help. I was also embarrassed at what I had just done. What I had just admitted.

Though my brain was fried, I had made a very conscious decision in that meeting: I did not mention my suicidal thoughts to them. Why? Because it's hard to talk about suicide, even if you're sure you wouldn't actually go through with it. And I felt sure I wouldn't actually go through with it. But so long as you had the thought, and there was at least a shred of seriousness to it, then it's hard to talk about. Hard to talk about with anyone—loved ones, colleagues, even (I imagined at that point) therapists. And it then put so much pressure on the person you told, to do something—*even when you knew you were not going to act on it.*

So imagine what it would be like to bring up the subject with the football coach or general manager who had just picked you to play for them.

I did not want anyone to overreact. I did not want some big intervention. I did not want to get cut. I did not want other people to find out. Who wants that stigma? I did not know what they would think of me. I was a brand-new player for them. I wondered if they already thought that they had made a mistake in picking me up off waivers—you know, just not worth the headache. So I said nothing about that part of it.

I had not told anyone. Not my parents. Not even Jill—not yet, anyway. How do you tell someone something that will alter their life? That you've had thoughts about ending *your* life? I didn't want to worry or burden her more than I already had.

In the car heading back to the hotel, I called my parents, who were driving from Buffalo to Baltimore to see me play. I told them I would not be playing in Sunday's game. I told them why. They immediately turned the car around and headed for Indianapolis.

I felt no embarrassment or stigma in telling my parents. I knew that they would understand it for what it was. Something was wrong with their son. He was sick. Nothing else mattered.

Later that day, I began taking Klonopin for the first time. It seemed to level some of the physical edge. It calmed my body down, lowered my heart rate—*seemed* to, anyway. It relaxed me. But it wasn't a "mind drug," at least not for me. I needed something else to help quiet my mind, slow the racing, anxious thoughts.

On Sunday, when I missed my first game with the Colts because of anxiety, insomnia, and other manifestations of my undiagnosed mental illness, the injury report for fans that scrolls along the bottom of the NFL Network and ESPN read:

. . . COLTS—KEITH O'NEIL—OUT—FLU . . .

I assumed that most people thought that going to a counselor, therapist, psychologist, psychiatrist, shrink, whatever you want to call it, was for the troubled, the weak, or the sick. Why did I assume this? Because that's how *I* thought for the longest time.

I was ready to let go of the preconception. I was excited about seeing a therapist. Maybe I would even come to call him or her "*my* therapist." I was open to anything and anyone that made me feel better. I imagined that a good therapist possessed the ability to open your mind and your heart to a world you did not know existed deep inside. Teach you a new way to think, react, even breathe.

Two days after the Ravens game, a Tuesday, I was eager for my first therapy session. Finally! Someone I could talk to about my issues, someone trained to understand and help. He was, I was told, a "sports psychologist affiliated with the team." He had worked with many top athletes from college and the pros. I drove to the medical plaza. As I entered his private office, I noticed that every inch of wall seemed to be covered with framed photographs of athletes, with the occasional diploma or certification thrown in. I sat down and immediately told him everything. My anxiety, my moods, even my childhood nickname, The Bear. I talked about my frequent, terrible bouts of insomnia going way back to when I was seven or eight years old and how it sometimes seemed unpredictable but tended to emerge when I felt under pressure.

"That's common, especially in sports," said the therapist. "Remember, you're playing at a high level and with that comes stress, which causes some people to have trouble sleeping."

"I know," I said, hoping there was more to his answer. There had to be. Maybe, in my exhaustion, I had missed some nuance. *Give him a chance, Keith.* "I think my situation is different, though. I can't shut my mind off. And I'm also very up and down a lot. I'm moody. I have a lot of anxiety about performance and stuff in general."

"There are ways for you to relax," he said without missing a beat. He was already done with the understanding part and onto the solution. "You need to find a way to relax yourself."

"I know, but this is different. *I'm* different. I've had suicidal thoughts before. I'm down a lot."

"Do you have suicidal thoughts now?"

"No," I lied.

"Good," he said, with finality. "I think you need to find ways to relax, to meditate on things before your performance. I'm going to give you a CD to listen to at night to help you relax and sleep."

"Okay," I said.

Wait . . . that was *it*? That's all a revelation of suicidal thoughts gets?

As the twenty-minute session ended, it's an understatement to say I was disappointed. I needed help, answers, a plan. I got nothing.

No, that's not true. As promised, he handed me a relaxation CD.

"Listen to this when you're lying awake at night," he instructed.

Yeah, this should do the trick, I thought. An Enya CD. Why didn't I think of that before?

I walked down the hall toward the main entrance to the complex. The "therapist" actually *had* accomplished something. He had inspired me to take bold action, or at least consider it: I really, really wanted to smash the CD against the wall.

~

I actually listened to it during the week. I did have some better nights of sleep. Eventually, though, I thought: *If I hear one more Enya track, I will truly lose my mind.*

Despite the way my time with the Colts started, I was able to push away the thoughts that made me seek out Coach Dungy that morning of the team flight to Baltimore. (We beat the Ravens, 24–7.) I practiced well during the week and suited up for the second game, at home against Jacksonville. Mom told me it took guts to go to Dungy and say I was sick— not sick with the flu but mentally sick—and that I needed help. She said it took unusual strength as a person. Dad said that throughout his whole career, playing and coaching, he had never heard of anyone doing that, because if a player *did* do that, he knew he would get cut. After all, the typical NFL career lasts only a couple years, if that, so you just shut up and go about your business if you want to keep your job.

For most of the season, my third in the league, I played the best football of my life for a team on an incredible roll. (We started the season winning our first 13 games, and finished 14–2, the #1 seed in the AFC.) I made some standout plays on special teams, including that dramatic Horizontal Mambo against the Tennessee Titans, and I was named special teams captain for multiple games, which was especially cool since I had been with the team for only a short while. I even got to play some linebacker (the Colts played a 4-3 defense, like the Cowboys used to). Not a lot but more than I had done for Dallas. Jill and I lived in a Marriott TownePlace Suite the entire season. While she and I were a bit homesick, my teammates were always gracious in opening their homes to us. Peyton Manning invited Jill and me to his home for Thanksgiving. I was accepted.

In late November, I again got nominated to be a squad captain for our Monday night home game against the Pittsburgh Steelers. Peyton served as captain for the offense, linebacker David Thornton for the defense, me for special teams. As we stood on the sideline right before walking out to midfield for the coin toss, Peyton leaned over to me and said, "O'Neil, you're calling the coin toss. What are you gonna call, heads or tails?"

"I'll call tails," I said.

"Okay," he said, "but make sure you tell the referee that you want to call tails *the second we get out there*. It's important! Don't forget!"

Walking to midfield, in front of a national television audience, all I could think about was that I had to tell the referee right away. We approached the Steelers' captains, shook hands, and as we prepared for the coin toss I leaned toward the ref and told him I wanted to call tails. He gave me an odd look. I told him again, thinking he might not have heard me. Again, an odd look. As the ref took out his coin, I leaned closer to him and said, "We call tails!"

The referee brushed me away, annoyed, and turned to the Steelers captains. "The Pittsburgh Steelers are the visiting team," said the ref into his microphone, then glared at me. "What do you call, heads or tails?"

I turned around to see Peyton and David Thornton laughing.

As I said: I felt accepted.

Pinned to a bulletin board in the Colts training complex, a flyer advertised a phone number you could call for "confidential" mental health help. I did not bother to write down the number.

Why should it be confidential?

Yeah, I know why but . . . why?

After all, being a little nuts hadn't affected my performance one bit. I could play great without my head being on
straight. Therefore, it shouldn't be shameful that I had this
mental problem, since I never took it out on the field with
me. (At least, if you ignore the Ravens game I missed.)

*Conduct yourself professionally for the week, then go be a
crazy man in public for three hours.*

*Go on the field and hit! . . . Now, get off the field and sit
quietly on the bench until the next play that involves kicking or
returning.*

I started to wonder if the NFL itself had a problem similar to
mine. After all, it rewarded recklessness and anger. And maybe
that fundamental fact is what kept it from too much self-exam-
ination. The league had a great out: *What you can't see on an MRI
or x-ray, you don't have to treat, diagnose, or even acknowledge.*

When an NFL player tells his team's appointed "sports
therapist" that he has had suicidal thoughts, something needs
to be done besides handing him a CD of ambient noise. (And
what does "sports therapist" even mean?)

Then again, what self-interest was there for a team—or
the league, for that matter—to explore what might be going
on in the psyche of one of its more troubled employees?
Especially if what was going on in his head might be a key
element in making him a useful weapon?

Suppose they had spent the time to figure me out. Suppose
they had diagnosed me correctly. Would I have lost my edge
and thus my value to the team? I'm in no position to suggest
that my mental state and my football value were two separate
issues. Maybe they were right to ignore it: It didn't relate to the
workplace. Grandpa Howdo had worked two jobs, including

his own business, for decades, without his mental issues seeming to affect the work he did.

And, hey: I was playing the best ball of my life. Maybe a happier, more stable Keith O'Neil would have been a professionally useless Keith O'Neil.

Then I got hurt. A broken sternum (first rib) and separated shoulder while busting the wedge during Week 5 versus the San Francisco 49ers. Afterward, the head equipment manager, one of the guys who had ignored me when I asked if I could get tighter shoulder pads, told me, "When you get healthy again, you're wearing *our* pads."

I missed six weeks.

When I finally returned, in Week 11 against the Cincinnati Bengals, I played just as well as I had before the injury.

Right after the regular-season finale against the Arizona Cardinals and before the first round of the playoffs, the team showed how much they truly believed in me: They offered me a two-year contract. Wow! The Colts did this *knowing* about my mental state (did they think it was all resolved from that one appointment?); they did it even with the significant physical injuries I had sustained during my brief time with them. I had the briefest conversation with Jack, my agent, about maybe playing the market, but quickly realized I would be nuts to do so. (Okay, a different kind of "nuts.") Though Indianapolis did not offer me a lot of money by football standards—it was again the league minimum plus a very welcome signing bonus of $125,000—I felt a loyalty to them and loved playing for them. Even if they had not cut me after the first "incident," they could have done so after my major physical injuries. But they didn't. Plus, I didn't want to go to another team and have to change again. I hated change.

Maybe, as my linebacker coach had said to me my first week with the team, I would stick around for a while.

~

I enjoyed the Colts culture. It didn't take me long to feel comfortable there. I loved Coach Dungy and the staff. He was great to work under, and always said: God first, family second, football third. That summed it up for him.

And he was a lot mellower than Coach Parcells. With Parcells, everyone was out at practice fifteen minutes early, at least, because no one dared to be late. My first practice at Indy, I went out to the field three minutes early . . . and no one was there, not even the equipment managers. I started to panic, thinking I had read the schedule wrong. I went back inside and waited for everyone else in the locker room. They were all late, even the staff.

When my Colts teammates and I went out to dinner, we often played a game called "credit card roulette": At the end of the meal we would each put a credit card in a hat and ask the waitress to pull out a card. Whoever's card got pulled had to pay the bill. My card got pulled once—eight hundred bucks for dinner—but I figured it all evened out in the end.

I created a Facebook page, posting photos and news and opinions about my life and work, a new way for me and others to communicate directly with fans.

Despite our 14–2 record, #1 seed, and first-round playoff bye, we got eliminated at home in the divisional round by the Steelers. In early 2006, after the season ended, I decided to get surgery on my shoulder. The doctors and trainers had all said it was my choice, that it was all based on pain tolerance, which only the individual can decide. I told Mr. Polian it was still bothering me and if I had surgery right after the season, I could be back in time for training camp, in good shape.

Even if there had been no surgery, it would have been a very busy offseason. Jill and I returned to Texas to get married. The wedding was a good illustration of the life of a pro football family. We married in Dallas, a city where we no longer lived, but planned it from Indianapolis, the city where I played, while I was from Buffalo and Jill, Arizona. We honeymooned in Tahiti, sold our house in Dallas, and bought a town house in Indianapolis.

My fourth year in the league promised to be a special football season. In high school, college, and my first three years in the NFL, I had had talented teammates and had played in playoff games, but I never felt as if we were clearly the class of that particular league. Going into the 2006 season, though, I knew we had the talent, experience, and depth to contend for a Super Bowl. Everyone knew it. We would build on and learn from the disappointing postseason of the year before. Now we just had to stay healthy and hope Peyton Manning's arm didn't fall off.

Throughout the season, I took sleep and anxiety meds when needed. When I was healthy, I played well. But after signing my two-year contract, it was my most injury-riddled season—high ankle sprain, sprained MCL, broken ribs. We finished the season 12–4 and again made the playoffs. Fortunately, I returned in time to play in the postseason, all the way through the Super Bowl.

The day before we left for Miami for the Super Bowl, my linebacker coach, Mike Murphy, a laid-back, good ol' boy who really knew his stuff and seemed to like me a lot, told us, "You guys have the chance to do something extremely special. Do you realize that there are only a handful of line-backers in the world with a Super Bowl ring? When we win next week, you'll all be part of that small fraternity." He gave all the linebackers a framed photograph of Secretariat, the legendary thoroughbred, coming down the straightaway at the Preakness Stakes, the final leg of the Triple Crown. In the picture, the jockey is looking back at the trailing horses, far behind in the distance. On each of the framed photos Murphy had written the date of the upcoming Super Bowl, February 4, 2007, and the words, "Remember the finish!"

"We have one game left to win," Murphy told us. He wasn't much for rah-rah or pregame speeches. "All we have to do is finish like Secretariat. Remember the finish."

In the days leading up to the game, I slept soundly every night. I practiced well. I was able to enjoy time with my teammates, and my family once they arrived in town. I played in the game with injuries that were still healing—ankle, ribs, MCL—plus freshly broken ribs in my back. But I didn't notice, truly. My mental state was clear and confi-dent. I played well, though I didn't make any tackles. There were some good blocks and I did not blow any assignments.

We beat the Chicago Bears in the pouring rain in Miami, 29–17.

It was beyond thrilling. I knew it was a rare opportunity to feel what it's like to reach the very top of your profession, if not your life.

But afterward, I wondered: *Why was I able to play that game—the highest-pressure contest in all of American sports—with zero anxiety? And then at other, quieter times the anxiety and fear all came flooding in?*

Did it depend on the *type* of pressure I felt?

For a long time I wondered how Super Bowl week panned out the way it did. Did I have the ability to control my mind and my illness? Was I in a state of what's called (I would learn later) euphoria-hypomania? I don't think so. How was it possible to play on the biggest stage in the world and have no symptoms? I felt no pressure, no anxiety, no racing thoughts, nothing. The mind does amazing things, both bad and good.

I did not realize at the time that it would be the last football game (that counted) I would ever play in.

A few months later, during OTAs in June, my groin was bothering me terribly. I saw a specialist in Philadelphia and he had me in surgery the next day. It was probably the biggest "physical" mistake of my career. I should have just sat out and rehabbed it rather than opting for surgery. Instead, because I missed so much of training camp, when I eventually got back I was in terrible shape. In our last preseason game, I broke another rib.

During final cuts—August 26, 2007, to be exact, my twenty-seventh birthday—I once again got a visit from The Turk. So my birthday would not just be the date my father got cut from the league, but the date I got cut, too.

When I was released, I got an "injury settlement," which was worth four weeks of regular season pay. The Colts originally said that, due to the severity of my injury, they would give me two weeks regular season pay since (by their estimation) that's how long it takes a rib to heal. Jack negotiated and came back with four weeks, and the Colts relented. Those extra two weeks I was being paid were huge—but not so much for the money it brought in immediately. If you are on an active roster or injured for at least three games in a year, you are credited with a season. Because Jack and I fought for those four weeks, it meant that I had a fifth active year in the NFL, and five years is a real threshold that helped with benefits like health insurance and pension kicking in. Still, I did not feel done with football.

Regardless of how I felt, football might have been done with me—and if a Super Bowl victory was the final game of my career, well, there were worse ways to go out.

Jill and I drove to Arizona and rented a condo so I could rehab for the following season. Roy Holmes, who had been a year ahead of me at NAU—he played safety—and whom I had always respected for his love of and dedication to the game of football, trained and pushed me back into playing shape. The following February, right after the Super Bowl, the New York Giants called. At my workout for them, I did the 40-yard dash, position drills, everything. They must have liked what they saw because they signed me to a one-year deal at the league minimum, which kicked in only if I made the team.

In the spring of 2007, Jill and I drove back East, where the Giants put us up, extended stay, at the Residence Inn by Marriott, in East Rutherford, New Jersey, right next to the stadium. At this point I should have been a stockholder in Marriott.

After going through a couple OTAs with the team, I realized that the fire had gone out.

It was more than that, though. I was mentally exhausted from my "condition." When not practicing with the Giants, I was extremely anxious. Of course I couldn't sleep. After an emotional conversation with Jill, I decided that I was going to retire once and for all.

But I wanted to go through one last practice.

I did everything to enjoy the moment; to enjoy practice like I never had my entire life, through all those times in high school where I just wanted to make it to the end. I reflected. Working out on the field right next to Giants Stadium, with a view of the Empire State Building in the distance, I couldn't help but think about what football had done for my family and me. From the places I'd been to the people I'd met to the lessons I'd learned. I thought about the struggle I had endured, both physically and mentally, and laughed about it to myself right there in the middle of the field. Out loud.

It's all going to be over after this practice. Forever.

Maybe some people who knew me might have thought I had quit the NFL, but you know what? If they did, then they really didn't know what I had been through. (And to be fair to them, maybe I hadn't been open enough about what I had been through.) My life and especially my football career had been an almost constant battle. To walk away after four-plus seasons in the NFL, with a Super Bowl ring on my finger, was good enough for me.

When the practice was over, I took a few final, very long inhales and exhales of the chilly spring air, wanting to breathe everything in one last time. Then I walked inside to the office of New York Giants head coach Tom Coughlin. I knocked on his door and entered.

"Coach, I know what it takes to make this football team. I don't have it in me anymore."

Coach Coughlin barely knew who I was. Still, he said something that I appreciated.

"I'm not going to try and talk you out of it since it appears you've made up your mind," he said. "I respect that you know what's best for you."

I thanked him for the opportunity, handed him my playbook, and retired for good.

It was bittersweet, made more so by the fact that, years before, I had been a ball boy for Rutgers when my father coached there and the Scarlet Knights played a couple of games each season at Giants Stadium. As a young boy I was in awe of these surroundings. Now, as I walked out of the stadium, I thought of scenes there from my childhood and everything in between. The full circle of it. I saw the tunnel to the parking lot, same now as it was then. The smell was as it had been twenty years before, or probably it was just my memory of it, the embedded aroma of wet hot dog buns, pretzels, New Jersey, and football. Back then, I dreamed of one day being a real player on that field someday.

Now I had.

Chapter 8

THE REAL SEASON STARTS

Jill and I, masters of the long road trip, drove back to Indianapolis, where we still had our place, to decide what to do with the rest of our lives. Return east, where I was from? Keep heading west, where Jill was from, where we had gone to school and met and fallen in love? After a couple of months deliberating, we chose my hometown of Buffalo. It was not an easy decision because we both loved Arizona. In Buffalo, though, we could be near my family. And because the area was more affordable, we could buy our dream home—a big brick Colonial on a spacious wooded lot, a stream running through it, in a very nice suburb called Clarence. The house had a deck. There was a gazebo.

The first few months there, Jill and I just enjoyed life. The house needed a total paint job and some other work, so we spent time on that. Then we traveled for an entire month to Europe—Amsterdam, Paris, Germany, Prague, Austria, Switzerland, and Italy. We ate great food, drank great wine, and met friendly, interesting people along the way. Then we visited Ka'aina and his family in Hawaii, saw places off the beaten path, swam on remote beaches, hiked remote trails, fished and ate what we caught, raw, right out of the ocean. When we returned to Buffalo, Kevin and I did something we had talked about for a long time: got tattoos. For me, on my right shoulder/arm, a Celtic cross with a red hand in the middle of it, symbol of Ulster, the county in Ireland where the O'Neils hailed from. Kevin's was similar.

Finally back home and without the discipline of football and the camaraderie of teammates, my endorphin release slowed to a crawl. I put on fifty pounds. I had spent my entire life working out and being in great shape, and now I wasn't working out at all.

I met up with an old friend at a local bar. From what I had previously heard from him, as well as from mutual friends in the interim, his alcohol and drug issues had worsened. Stupidly, I went off, telling him he needed to straighten out.

I meant well. I cared deeply for him and his family. I considered him a close friend. Big deal.

He looked at me once I'd finished. "What about you?" he said. "Look at you. *Your* life's over. You're done with the NFL. The best part of your life is over. You're nothing now."

In December 2008, I got a job as a sales associate at a company that sold sports medicine implants and other equipment to doctors who repaired ACLs, MCLs, and the meniscus (all knee-related), rotator cuffs and labrums (shoulder), biceps, and more, injuries all very common to football. My brother and brother-in-law also worked in the industry. It was another frequently high-stress job but I loved it . . . at least at first. As a sales rep, my days were spent assisting surgeons and their staff in the proper use of the equipment—making sure it was all sterile and ready to go in the operating room, and having all the proper-sized, proper-shaped implants. During surgery, I had to be available to answer any questions the doctor might have. (Often there were none, but once I actually had to guide the surgeon on the use of my company's instruments and techniques, from first step to completion on an ACL repair. I had not realized a surgeon could be so clueless.) My responsibilities also included dealing with billing the hospital, setting up lunches to promote our wares to medical personnel, organizing classes for surgeons to familiarize themselves with our products, maintaining inventory, and keeping up to date on new trials. I had a great rapport with my immediate boss, who seemed to have much to teach me, not only about the business, but also about how life could be after football.

Jill, who is incredibly good at what she does wherever she does it, soon got a job as a registered nurse at the Women and Children's Hospital of Buffalo. She was given the most intense assignment: pediatric intensive care unit and ER. I could never have done what she did.

A short time after, I got another tattoo: Under my left arm, they inked 35°13' N 111°67' W, coordinates of Flagstaff, where I overcame a lot and which would always have a place in my heart.

While I was settling into my new job and Jill into hers, on August 26, my birthday, we received the most amazing news: Jill was pregnant! No longer was that date tainted by being the one that two O'Neils had their football careers end. Now it was the magical date we found out we were going to be parents. We revealed the news to my whole family at Kevin's son's baptism. We called for everyone's attention, and I put my arm around Jill and asked someone to "take a picture . . . of the three of us," as I moved my hand gently over Jill's stomach. Everyone was overjoyed.

New jobs that we both loved, back home living in our dream house near family, on the verge of having our first child. The stressors and uncertainties of playing in the NFL retreating in the rearview.

Life was good. For the first time in our lives, in fact, everything was perfect.

It happened at nine weeks.

I was at work when Jill called about the miscarriage. The news upset me, of course, but I managed to finish delivering some medical equipment, then preparing the instruments that needed to go out the next day. I hurried home to find Jill in the bathroom, very emotional. I wouldn't say I felt emotional as much as empty.

The next day, my mother told me she was driving my grandmother, who had been visiting in Buffalo, back home to Michigan.

Something inside me snapped.

I had never had a real, loud argument with Mom before, and here I was screaming at her. I was hurt and pissed that she would leave Jill and me the day after our miscarriage.

The O'Neil Kids in 1982: Kevin, Colleen, and Keith. I'm two years old in this photo, on the left.

Me at three years old, 1983.

HOWELL CENTRAL

1990

My first love: baseball. Me at ten years old. Would anyone know I was battling demons at such a young age?

My first years of football, at age thirteen, with the Howell Lions in eighth grade.

With my dad, enjoying time together the week before I leave for college at NAU, 1999.

The family on the practice field at NAU, with the San Francisco Peaks in the background.

With Ka'aina after a NAU victory. My Hawaiian brother from another mother.

With Jill the day I was notified by the Cowboys that they were signing me, at my college apartment in Flagstaff, Arizona.

The entire family at Drew's UB Hall of Fame induction: Me, Jill, Mom, Dad, Colleen, Drew, Jill (Kevin's wife), and Kevin.

With Jill the day we told the family we were pregnant with our first child.

My first regular season game with the Cowboys, against the Atlanta Falcons, September 7, 2003. I actually dislocated my pinkie finger on my first-ever NFL tackle on punt coverage.

The happy couple on our wedding day.

Action shot—look at that focus!

The captains: Peyton Manning, Gary Brackett, and me walking out for the pre-game coin toss.

With Rocky Boiman (my boy) celebrating after the AFC Championship game on January 21, 2007. "We're going to the Super Bowl!"

On punt coverage, trying to stay dry during Super Bowl XLI, February 4, 2007.

My entire family supporting me before Super Bowl XLI.

The family celebrating after our Super Bowl victory. We're world champions!

"Tears of Joy," as Jill and I share a special moment on the field after the Super Bowl victory.

Celebrating with my teammates in the locker room after winning the Super Bowl.

With the Lombari Trophy after our victory, showing off my child-like excitement.

With Coach Dungy and the Lombardi Trophy after the big win.

Ugly Christmas Sweater Party with my Colts teammates. I won best costume for dressing up as Ralphie from the film *A Christmas Story*.

With Jill at the Super Bowl Ring Ceremony.

Hiking the Grand Canyon with Coach Lees, Jimmy, and CR, May 2016.

With Jill and my favorite band of all time, 311. Guitarist Tim Mahoney and drummer Chad Sexton were nice enough to take this shot with us. Meeting them that night was (almost) as good as winning a Super Bowl!

With my older son Connor enjoying a laugh, 2013.

With Connor, hiking in Sedona, Arizona. One of my favorite pictures.

With Jill and Connor at Christmas, 2015.

Tossing Connor in the air at the NAU practice fields.

With my younger son Tanner at a BBQ, summer 2016.

Over and over I kept saying, "I should have moved to Arizona when I had the chance." We had moved to Buffalo, not out west, which for several reasons we would have preferred, to be around my family. Now here they were, abandoning us, as I perceived it, right when something bad happened and we could have used the support.

I did not know what to do to make things better for Jill, for me, for us. I felt lost. I felt I had no control over the situation.

You know who or what had control? The miscarriage. The miscarriage somehow became the trigger for my descent into hell. The trigger was a loss, not an injury. Actually, as a doctor would point out later, the trigger was *two* losses: the next generation (miscarriage) and the previous generation (Mom "leaving").

Just days after the devastating news about the pregnancy, I felt like I was on Cloud Nine.

That's not a typo. You read that right.

What the hell?

Jill had just suffered a heartbreaking calamity, both physical and psychological. Yet in just the few days of feeling empty over the miscarriage, compounded by anger and betrayal that my mother was leaving town, I felt my emotions do a U-turn.

I was euphoric. I thought everything in life was great. I became very motivated and goal-oriented. I started to work eighteen-hour days, countless hours in my office, at least some of which should have been spent comforting my wife and grieving with her over the loss of our unborn child.

I was sleepless, but felt in control. I was like a car engine that was racing. I worked more and more.

While driving, I thought to myself how good I felt and how I couldn't shut up, whether or not anyone else was around. I was self-aware, but didn't think anything was wrong. I listened to music loud, often my favorite band, 311. I particularly loved the song, "From Chaos."

From chaos comes clarity, I tell ya
What you appear to be, you ought to know
Glycerin tears don't fool me, I tell ya
Delusions plaguing everybody
. . . It's not something you can fake, son
You're a con man whose run is done
You lead a world wide web of deception . . .

I listened to music very loud and drove very fast. I felt invincible, on top of the world.

If I'm being totally honest? I felt . . . happy.

Your wife miscarries and you feel happy.

At home, I talked Jill's ear off, 100 mph. *I love my job, I'm so good at my job, I could be the CEO one day . . . I have so many ideas for work but I don't want to tell people or they'll steal them . . . I slept four hours last night, that's plenty for me, I feel great! I love my life!*

When I had a break or after work, I sometimes dropped by my parents' house and talked my mother's ear off. As selfish as I was, and as oblivious as I often was to Jill's sadness, I figured it wasn't fair to her that she be the only one to hear me go on and on. Mom probably thought my behavior was a little odd, or maybe that I was genuinely happy at work.

Then, just as abruptly, I crashed. All I could do was lie on the couch and sleep. It was obvious to Jill and me that something was wrong. I began to research my symptoms online. I diagnosed myself with Cyclothymia, a mild form of bipolar disorder.

Jill and I both knew something was deeply wrong with me—yet maybe we didn't trust that it was enough to raise a red flag . . . and before I knew it, just days later, I was manic again. Suddenly, my self-diagnosis was shoved to the back of the closet.

Again, I had boundless energy. I worked and worked. I came up with crazy ideas for the company. My immediate boss and I had lunch with a surgeon and a top executive. The executive and I clicked right away, or so I thought, and I began sending him my ideas—at 3 a.m. Lying in bed at night, concocting new techniques for knee surgery (that's right, me, a sales rep, fresh out of the NFL, who had zero background in performing surgery), I would email the executive from my phone. I emailed him ideas on how to use social media as a tool to promote our surgeons. I volunteered to speak to new hires about what it was like to be a sales rep. Grandiose thinking! It felt important. I felt important.

Everything I did that felt good fed the mania, making me more manic. It was a drug: The more you do, the more you want to do. Everywhere I went, whether to work or the store, my confidence soared. Everything seemed interesting—music, politics, religion, astronomy, *everything*. I was selling equipment to surgeons like never before. I was charming and outwardly happy. (The Bear? Charming and outwardly happy?) I talked fast, my thoughts a white-hot jumble. I couldn't stop.

Then I went on a ridiculous shopping spree. It started with clothes, which I never bought for myself (Jill mostly bought my clothes). I went to a higher-end shopping plaza and bought a couple pairs of designer jeans, some shirts, an expensive jacket. I felt great. I felt "sexy" for the first time in my life. I thought people cared how I looked. *I* cared, which was strange because I never had before. One morning I put on a pair of new designer jeans and a new button-down shirt, all to go to the grocery store. Taken aback, Jill asked, "Where are you going?" Normally I would have been in a hoodie and sweat pants.

I wasn't finished spending—not even close. I took Jill to a jewelry store near our home. We were there to swap her diamond earrings for a new pair, an upgrade of maybe a couple hundred bucks. As soon as I walked into the store, though, all I noticed were the watches. I saw the Rolex. Price tag, eleven grand. *That's nothing*, I thought to myself. *I can afford that.* (No, I really couldn't.) I saw a black Tag Heuer, a mere thousand bucks. I convinced Jill that I deserved them. The state I was in, I could have sold anything to anyone. *We deserve this*, I kept saying. *All the hard work we put in in the NFL. I never buy anything. It's time for me to treat myself. Us.*

I asked Jill what she wanted. She had not expected that. We had come to upgrade her earrings, a relatively cheap job. But I caught her looking at two pairs of diamond earrings.

"Get both," I suggested.

She was shocked. She refused. But I would not be talked out of it. I was a great salesman. She tried to make counter-arguments, with no luck. "They can be for our anniversary," I rationalized.

"Last year you took me to Olive Garden," she said. Finally, she agreed to accept one pair of diamond earrings, not both.

From the jewelry store I called my financial advisor to make sure I had enough cash in my checking account to cover everything. Two watches, a pair of diamond stud earrings, fifteen thousand bucks total.

I was not finished. Three days later I decided we needed a hot tub in our backyard. I made Jill come to the pool store with me. I thought I was so cool, that I was selling the pool salesman instead of him selling me. Here I was, ex-NFL, rising medical device sales superstar. He had nothing on me.

He totally sold me. Idiotically, I made it plain up front that I did not care about the price tag. I ended up buying a top-of-the-line hot tub. With installation and taxes, ten thousand bucks.

We would never use it. Not once.

The day after the hot tub, I bought more clothes, enough to call it a new wardrobe. The day after that, two snowboards, plus all the bells and whistles that go with them. I went to a store that sold all sorts of safes because I suddenly believed I needed a place to secure my Super Bowl ring and our other valuables and important paperwork. I ended up buying a "shotgun safe" (price tag: seven hundred dollars) that was so big, Kevin had to help me carry it upstairs to my bedroom closet. I bolted it to the floor. Oh, and despite its name, I didn't even own a shotgun, or a gun of any kind.

A week after buying the Rolex, I realized I didn't want it anymore. I went back to the jewelry store to return it but they would only give me store credit. Then and there I used five thousand of it to buy Jill the other pair of diamond earrings she had looked at.

Having dropped thirty thousand dollars during a week-long shopping spree, I now turned my attention to other things I absolutely *had* to accomplish. I sent very detailed, aggressive emails to NAU's athletic director and sports information director saying that the head football coach needed to be fired. Then I called some of the school's top donors about getting the coach fired. I talked Jill's ear off about it, naturally. I wanted to have my father installed as coach. I had the entire staff picked out, including his new linebacker/special teams coach: me. My whole family could all live together in Flagstaff.

Very soon after, I deeply regretted sending the emails and making the calls. I didn't really want to get the coach fired.

I was a model of impulsiveness and impatience. I cleaned the house, exercised, continued writing down my nonstop, insane ideas. When I listened to music on my headphones, it couldn't possibly sound any better than it did. It felt as if every instrument was running through my body.

And there was my wife, in great emotional pain. Grieving.

I felt productive, constructive—but anxiety was mixed in as well. This was the upside of obsessiveness—but it was still obsessiveness. Mostly, I was completely in my own head, all but indifferent to what Jill was going through. In her words, I was "locked in my world." Not that I knew or cared. Lack of empathy is a major trait of being locked in your world.

Then, after two weeks of this, and as abruptly as it started, my euphoria and hypermotivation turned dark. Paranoia. I heard voices. I was scared to death, pacing, sweating profusely, filled with anxiety. At home I followed Jill everywhere, rambling. She remained calm and strong, her training as a nurse kicking in. But she didn't know exactly what to do. Given the unpredictability of my condition, how could she?

More mania and paranoia. Not only was Corporate America full of nothing but cheaters and liars, I decided, but virtually every colleague of mine was using me because I was a Super Bowl champ. I was suspicious of what they *really* thought of me.

The biggest issue in the world for me, for a while, was this: In the email I had sent to the athletic director of NAU, I had misspelled the name of the coach I had tried to get fired. *How oh how could I correct that terrible mistake?*

A week or so before Christmas, I went to Best Buy to purchase a DVD, a gift for one of my nephews. Within seconds of entering the store I grew extremely paranoid. I was sure that all the employees were watching me. I spent a half-hour unsuccessfully searching for the DVD. I began to worry that I would forget what I was looking for and why I was there to begin with. I became certain that one employee in particular was following me, so I left quickly without buying what I had come for. Back in the car, sitting in the mall parking lot, I thought, *Should I be driving?*

That night, in our guest bedroom, I was speaking on the phone with my boss's boss, explaining what was "going on" with me. I did not care about the ramifications of being so candid (clearly). I told him everything. I didn't know how not to. I sent him a letter to explain things in more detail. He seemed supportive of me and what I was telling him—until Human Resources got involved and sent me a "corporate workplace email."

When I got it, I started pacing (though I was probably pacing before I got it). "Jill, why did I send that letter? Do you think they read it? What are they doing? What did I do? Do you think they're meeting about it? Oh my God! What should I do? Should I write another one?"

I had to fill out a form from HR. I needed Jill by my side. "Jill, why is HR sending me an email? Do they know what's going on with me? Can they read my computer, my phone? Help me answer these questions. My computer is bugged. Unplug it! I need to unplug all the wires. They can read everything."

Jill assured me that my computer was not bugged. No matter: I unplugged it and disconnected all the wires and cables, then plugged them all back in. I was locked in paranoia. I paced the house. Thousands of thoughts going through my head, thousands of words coming out of my mouth.

"Jill, people are listening in on my conversations."

"Like who, Keith? You're acting paranoid."

"They can read all my texts. They know what I'm saying."

I went from thinking my phone and computer were bugged to believing my brain and thoughts were bugged by the powers above, the airwaves, an extreme being—whoever they were, they were listening. They wanted to get in my head. I could feel them. I did things and believed things I never would have in a stable condition.

Our home, with all the upgrades we'd made to it in the months after we'd moved in, had always been a source of contentment. Now, I hated it. I told myself I didn't need the house. It was too big. Too nice.

That night, with Jill's guidance, I emailed a friend's mother, a psychologist, and made an appointment to see her the following day. When Jill and I arrived at her office, I was in a relatively stable condition. We all agreed that I needed to see a psychiatrist who could properly diagnose me and prescribe medication, if necessary. The first psychiatrist I was recommended didn't have availability for a month. I couldn't wait that long. The second choice could see me in six days, so I made an appointment. Somehow, I believed that nothing worse could transpire over the next few days—as if my condition would give me a break, as if it was under my control, now that I had respected it enough to address it seriously. At home that evening, my phone rang. MARK, it read on my phone's screen. The name and number of an old, trusted friend from high school.

Is it really *Mark?* I thought.

Our conversation centered around a Christmas party that Jill and I were planning, and whether I was going to invite a certain mutual friend. While we talked, I became convinced that the airwaves in my phone were listening to my mind. I hustled Mark off the conversation, rudely. By the time the call ended, I was at the door of my house, then I was outdoors in the freezing cold, running down the middle of my street, trying to get the airwaves to stop reading my thoughts. I was wearing just my sweats, on a late December night in Buffalo, New York. The problem, I realized (*How dumb! Why did I not think of it before?*), was with the *phone*, which I still had on me, so I flung it while sprinting down our quiet, snow-covered suburban street, into a bush covered with snow.

Dumb mistake, I thought. *Dumb, dumb, dumb.* I stopped, ran back, and dropped to my hands and knees to search through the snow for my phone.

The next couple days I continued to follow Jill around the house, like her shadow. She didn't know what to do about me or for me. Should she take me to the hospital? To the psychiatrist? Call my parents? She just gritted her teeth and dealt with it as best she could. On Christmas Eve I fell asleep at 9:30 p.m., then slept until 9:30 in the morning, Christmas Day. At least I woke to a day where I wasn't obsessing— though it was hard to take much comfort in this since I had no idea why one day was more tolerable than the previous one, or maybe the next one would be. There was a huge element of randomness to it.

The next afternoon, I lay in bed with my headphones on, trying to meditate, to get the chaos to stop . . . when I saw my brain coming out of my forehead. But it didn't look like a real brain. It was a digital brain. The only salvation was that

I was aware, somewhat aware, that I was hallucinating. Probably hallucinating. I snatched the headphones off and threw them to the floor. I rolled over to Jill's empty side of the bed. The entire bed was soaked from my sweat. As I lay there, God began to speak to me. I didn't hear His voice—but He was talking to me, I felt His presence, He was in my body. I felt like a prophet. I *was* a prophet. I was being called by Jesus to be a prophet. I did not hear any actual words calling me but I *felt* warmth and euphoria. In my mind I saw and felt the colors white and gold.

You are my prophet. Go spread the word.

That night, while sitting on the edge of the bathtub while Jill was doing her hair, I realized I couldn't wait for the visit to the psychiatrist and told her to take me to the hospital.

Chapter 9

DIAGNOSIS

"What is actually observed in so-called 'bipolar children?' If you read the research reports carefully, they describe broad and persistent emotional dysregulation. Although these children have mood swings, they do not develop manic or hypomanic episodes. They are moody, irritable, oppositional, and likely to misbehave—like all children with disruptive behavior disorders. Their grandiose thinking usually consists of little beyond boastfulness. No evidence from genetics, neurobiology, follow-up studies, or treatment response shows that this syndrome has anything in common with classical bipolarity."

—Joel Paris,
The Intelligent Clinician's Guide to the DSM-5

Looking back, I'm glad Jill didn't listen to me. Her judgment was impeccable, even if I didn't trust it, or her, or anything.

She could see I was freaking out. But had she listened to me, I probably would have ended up in the psychiatric hospital for an extended stay. Who knows what else?

Throughout my descent into paranoia, Jill had been in regular touch by phone with the therapist that I had so recently started seeing. Now, Jill called her to say that we couldn't wait even the couple more days to see the scheduled psychiatrist. We needed one *now*. The therapist got us an appointment with a psychiatrist the next day.

On the drive over to the office, I argued with Jill the whole time. I thought she was going the wrong way, which is funny since I had no idea the address of the office.

I stared out the window at the snow. I was still worried about the email I had written to the Athletic Director at NAU, the tapping of phones and computers, and my mind. Misspellings.

"Hurry up, we're going to be late!" I said, agitated, to Jill. "We're going the wrong way! Turn around! We passed the office!"

"Keith, relax. No, we're not going the wrong way. I know where I'm going. We won't be late. And quit worrying about the letter. You're overreacting."

"Make sure you tell the doctor everything that's going on with me," I said, my face pressed against the car window, staring out at white and grey, ground and sky, people and cars and boxy buildings and roads. "Please. You have to tell her everything."

"I will. Relax."

We got there on time, of course. We walked through endless snow to get to the office door. We sat in the waiting room, quietly, and I tried to keep from growing too agitated while Jill filled out the paperwork because I was incapable. Everything was scaring me. It was so quiet in the waiting room, empty except for us and the secretary. We kept making eye contact, she and I. She knew exactly why I was there. Yeah, she knew. Why was Jill taking forever to complete the paperwork? "Stop, we can finish it later, let's just go see the doctor," I said to her, over and over, like a chant.

Scared as I was generally, I wasn't scared to see the doctor. I *wanted* to see her. I wanted help. I wanted to find out what was going on.

Finally, the doctor stepped out of the hallway and I quickly stood. I suddenly felt fear. To be honest, I was frightened to death. But I was also eager. I bolted to her office—a bit too quickly, as Jill and the doctor had to lead me out of the wrong room and bring me to the right one.

As we sat in the doctor's office, I had my head angled back against the window and the heat from my body steamed it up. I stared out the window at the falling snow. Though I was terrified, I tried my hardest to remain calm while Jill and the doctor did all the talking. It was so hard, maintaining the calm. But I didn't say a word. I was overwhelmed to be there, so out of touch.

The doctor diagnosed me as having Bipolar I disorder, and being "in a mixed state," which meant that I had symptoms of both mania and depression—though I'm not sure I took it all in at the time. I know that's what was said because Jill would tell me later, and again and again. Still, I remember looking down at the doctor's desk as I walked out of the office and seeing the word "bipolar" written on a sheet of paper.

I had known for some time that this diagnosis was possible. Cyclothymia, which I had self-diagnosed, was a mild form of bipolar disorder. What I had was more severe. And seeing it in ink, the black scrawl on a doctor's pad, made it real. I was scared of what it actually meant, being bipolar. How it was going to change my life.

I should have known by then that things were just beginning. That my nightmare was just beginning.

~

After the appointment, Jill and I headed to a pharmacy to pick up the medication I had been prescribed—Geodon (anti-psychotic), Depakote (mood stabilizer), and Klonopin (anti-anxiety). The only pharmacies that existed, I knew for sure, were Walgreens and CVS. They were the only ones in the world. Jill pulled into a Target. We walked in, all the way to their "pharmacy."

No wonder they were out of one of the medications I needed.

"Target isn't a real pharmacy," I told Jill. "It's a supermarket. It's a department store. It's not a pharmacy." As we drove around and around Buffalo to find the medication, I told Jill that the doctor had sent us to Target to play a trick on me.

Because of the terrible shape I was in, we decided to spend the night at my parents' house. Not surprisingly, no one knew how to handle me, or the situation. Everyone was uncomfortable. My parents asked me about the medication I had just picked up and had started taking that evening, but I found the conversation overwhelming, like everything else at that point. Not helpful. Talking about the situation didn't make it easier. Not talking about it also didn't help—yet I felt I could not *not* talk about it. It was the only thing on my mind. I tried to watch TV but couldn't pay attention.

To distract us all, Dad thought it would be a good idea to go look at Christmas lights. Had it not been such an unfunny time, there was something funny about it: four adults going to look at Christmas lights. Who does that without little kids? Dad drove and I sat shotgun, with Jill and Mom in the back. I was hyperaware of things that weren't that important, like where everyone was sitting (Jill behind me, Mom behind Dad) and not at all aware of things that were, like where I was. I didn't know if it was the new drugs, the side effects, my illness, or some mixture of everything but it felt as if the bipolar was being pulled through me. *The Bipolar.* That's how I saw it and felt it. *The.* It was as if someone was grabbing my spine and pulling it, The Bipolar, out of my neck. I was in pain. I sat in the front seat holding Jill's hand behind me, shaking uncontrollably.

"My skin is crawling off," I said. "My skin is crawling off." I said it over and over, a new chant.

My parents and Jill remained calm, though they were obviously terrified. Other than the pain and confusion, the only thing I was aware of was the sound when my father auto-locked the doors to the truck. I guess he was afraid I might jump out. We pulled up to a house with an elaborate light display. If you tuned your car radio to the right station, the lights on the house flickered in sync with the music. It was a very old house, in an old town just north of Buffalo—or at least I thought it was. The house was white. On one side of the street was a large creek. Christmas songs came over the radio. We watched them flicker on and off, the colored lights, in different bunches and patterns, watched them through the car windows, fogged from my body heat, the music pounding through my body so hard that it hurt. I held Jill's hand over my left shoulder.

I woke up early the next morning. Dad was up, but Jill and Mom were still sleeping. I felt better than the night before, but the anxiety had not subsided. Damn. I was hoping for a miracle. Why shouldn't I? Later in the day, as things got a little clearer, I would feel more and more embarrassment about how I had acted in front of people who knew me and those who did not. But now, it felt as if things had begun to slow a bit, which was good. The medication seemed to have knocked the mania out of me. But I could not stop worrying about what I had just gone through and how I was going to handle work now that I had been officially diagnosed with bipolar disorder. There was no turning back, was there? You made the team or not. You broke the plane of the goal line or not. You are pregnant or not. You are bipolar or not. I could not stop pacing the house for what seemed like hours. Dad tried to calm me, reassuring me that everything was okay; that I was going to be okay.

Then the anxiety took over. It was an anxiety attack. I started to rock back and forth on my feet. I couldn't breathe—or at least it felt that way. My heart was pounding out of my chest. It felt as if it was going to break through. My father, from behind, bear-hugged me. I could not see the look on his face.

He held on but I was out of control. Two ex-NFL line-backers. He held me tight, tight. We were just a couple of feet from a glass door leading to the backyard deck, and I thought about smashing my head into the glass. *That would help, right?* I thought. *Make things easier. At least change how it is right now, right?* My father held tighter. I wonder if he could tell that I was thinking about smashing my head through the glass. Probably, is my guess. Finally, the anxiety felt as if it was lifting. It lifted. It was lifting. I could feel it lifting out of me.

Night: 8p. 60mg Geodon
11p. w + 1000mg Depakote

12/29 day: 8a. 60 mg Geodon — made him sleepy
7p. 60mg Geodon "rough day"
11p. 1000 mg Depakote
* With agreeing c̄ KO 3 just being @ "better
We haven't argued at all. call"
12/30 day: Slept till alarm @ 630a.m

At the recommendation of the psychiatrist, Jill started to keep a journal of my behavior and medication intake.

A week after I was diagnosed with Bipolar I disorder, I made my first solo trip to the pharmacy.

On the way there, I realized that I had never actually been to one before. Sure, I had been to a Walgreens but I had never visited a pharmacy to get medication until the week prior, when I was sure that our trip to Target was a trick. I was thirty years old and this was the first time I had gone by myself to a drugstore. Until then, medication was provided by my team doctor, before that by my parents. Yeah, kind of shielded.

When I walked into the drugstore, the intense delusions and hallucinations of the week before were gone (or so I thought), but the other symptoms were not—some mania, anxiety, confusion, a general feeling of being overwhelmed. I was slowly adapting to the anti-psychotics and mood stabilizers.

I hoped I didn't run into someone I knew.

As I approached the pharmacy counter, I thought everyone in the store knew I was bipolar. Every customer and employee was staring at me, and the people standing in line could hear my heart beat. I was sweating. Everyone noticed the sweat rolling down the sides of my face. Facing the pharmacist, I was sure she knew why I was there. "They" had told her. She had been waiting for me.

I leaned over the counter, the pharmacist leaned toward me, and I whispered, "Can my wife come get my meds?"

"Yes," said the pharmacist, with a kind smile.

I was out the door in seconds.

For the foreseeable future, Jill would be the one to pick up my medicine.

~

Having a clear diagnosis should have answered a lot of questions for me. Yet the biggest feeling of all was disbelief.

That's what I have? That's who I am? That's what's been in control all these years?

Though I had suspected it for some time, I wouldn't believe it. Something was there, obviously, but the concept of this mental illness, the truth of it, felt to me like a caged animal desperately wanting to flee. It didn't belong inside me.

Get The Bipolar out.

Get out.

That's when my therapist "comforted" me that bipolar was something I had, not something I was.

Bipolar disorder is an illness, that's all, I told myself. *Bipolar isn't you.*

My employer had put me on short-term disability but the new psychiatrist I was seeing kept asking me, "Are you ready to go back to work?"

I didn't think so. I told her so. There were apparently all kinds of behaviors to consider, to change. Any alcohol I drank would "trump anything else processed in the liver," so I had better lay off. Did I need to go to AA? Would it change things if I went?

Caffeine was a "don't."

What if I took a vitamin D supplement, since you can't get any sunlight during a Buffalo winter?

What if I quit tobacco? I had dipped since I was nineteen, and was a very occasional social smoker. Would that make any difference?

Something else that needed to change: I had trouble redirecting my thoughts when they started to go off the rails. I could go an entire day thinking about one thing, or I could think about a thousand things. I could be obsessed about my obsessing. "Regular" obsession was tough enough on Jill, but obsession about obsession made it almost unbearable. The first, you're in a maze and you're trying to get at some out-of-the-way piece of cheese. The second you're in a maze, period. No goal to satisfy, just . . . stuck.

There was still more to fix. I knew I could get emotional very quickly. Maybe not ideal, especially for a guy (for how people perceive you, I mean, not for how I personally felt about being emotional). The key was: Once I got emotional, could I also be levelheaded? At the same time?

Then I told the psychiatrist I wanted to get back to work, and she agreed that I was ready. But I was clearly not, and she never should have signed off on it. Her solution to my problems was to increase my antidepressant dosage.

I should not have encouraged her to let me get back to work, but I needed the distraction. Part of me feared that if I didn't return soon, others would figure out what was wrong with me. Jill tried to talk me out of working, but my worry about being found out overrode her concern or any other concern I had or should have had. She couldn't stop me.

Granted: It wasn't the world's best idea. After all, if I had not felt such pressure to work, I could easily have slept fifteen hours straight, every night, from a combination of depression and medication. That doesn't sound like the best mindset and body for being in an OR during surgery.

But I was swimming in uncharted waters with no idea what to do. I felt it was Me vs. Bipolar. I was the one making the ultimate decisions, not my doctor, not Jill, no one.

I went back to work.

I could tell that my boss was concerned by my quick return, but he was reluctant to say anything because he didn't know how. I felt for him, since there were so many things *I* didn't know how to say. At first, he was timid around me. Then, when I felt comfortable enough to do it, about two weeks after my return, I told him all that was going on. He did not know what to do except to assign me fewer cases, and more straightforward ones. He didn't make me do anything else—selling, going to lunches, or taking (or leading!) courses.

I tried hard to act "normal" at work, but it was difficult. Even with a significantly reduced caseload, the day-to-day remained extremely stressful. There were times in the operating room where I was just praying that the surgeon or staff would not call on me for assistance. But of course, things happened. In one case, a surgeon had trouble with the "endobutton," a key device in the ACL reconstruction he was performing. I offered a suggestion, though I had no clue what the problem was. Afterward, the surgeon told me that my job was to assist the scrub techs, not tell him how to do surgery.

Yet I often obsessed about being undercompensated. I often felt disgust toward people at work, and people in general.

As a sales rep, I still had responsibilities to speak in public, so I took a training session with Toastmasters. As if the next speech of mine, at some national sales conference, wasn't a guaranteed disaster waiting to happen.

Jill had long put the responsibility of taking care of me and getting me better all on herself. She was very unhappy that I was back at work.

Over the first several months of 2011, the meds I'd been given did as much harm as good, taking a toll on me both mentally and physically. The side effects—anxiety, drowsiness, weight gain—sometimes seemed worse than the illness itself. The drugs knocked out the mania but it was replaced by deep depression and an intensity to my anxiety that surpassed anything I'd felt when struggling in the NFL, or as a boy. This was way worse.

Once upon a time, I could not sleep no matter what I did. I prayed and begged for sleep. Now it was a struggle to stay awake.

The psychiatrist prescribed Cymbalta, an antidepressant, and soon after upped the dosage.

For quite some time after the original diagnosis, I would make Jill go with me to all my psychiatrist and psychologist appointments. I could not function properly. My memory was shot and I wouldn't be able to retain the information during the session. Was that why the meetings with the psychiatrist were only fifteen minutes long, and only once every six weeks? That didn't seem right. I was in terrible shape. I needed more time and attention. But the doctor I'd been assigned was too "busy."

The worst of the depression lasted for half a year, through the middle of 2011. When I wasn't working, I slept. For six months, like a hibernating bear. I barely ate, bathed, brushed my teeth, or even drank water. Aside from going on my occasional work assignments, I hardly left the house. It didn't help that the start of my depression coincided with the endless, unforgiving Buffalo winter. Sunlight was minimal. I craved it and on sunny days I would open the front door and lie on the floor just inside the entrance to our home, in the sunlight, like a dog. Curled up in the warm spot, I could sleep there for hours.

My immediate family wanted to help, but I didn't let them because I didn't know how. I was learning to live with my newly diagnosed illness and its symptoms, as well as the insecurities that came with it. Nothing they could do would really benefit me, I decided, and there was no way that they understood. I kept the news of my illness a secret from everyone else—extended family and other friends. I didn't want anyone to know because I was scared and I was sick.

Depression is real, I understood all too well. It is not a mental weakness. It is not just laziness or character deficiency or an inability to do what you know needs doing. It is not "just" anything. It is chemical, and it needs to be addressed.

It is distinct from anxiety, which is a different sort of debilitating. Anxiety is being nervous for a big speech or a big game, only all the time, and multiplying fast in its intensity, its ability to paralyze you. Fast heart rate, mind racing, nervousness— boundless fear.

Depression is sleeping because you'd rather do that than face the day. Every day. And immediately upon waking, feeling sorry that you woke. That you ever woke.

Early one March morning, several months into this intense depression, my parents came over to the house. I cried on their shoulders for no specific reason I could name. This was depression.

Everything felt overwhelming. Life was overwhelming. On the rare occasions when Jill and I went out together to a restaurant, she had to pay the bill because I could not calculate the tip. It was too much for me to do even simple math.

Anyway, it was embarrassing for me to be in public because of how uncontrollably my hands shook from the medication.

The one thing I felt I could do, that I could control, was to get to know my illness.

I spent hours a day on the Internet, obsessing over my illness. I googled everything: bipolar disorder, bipolar work, bipolar jobs, bipolar treatment, bipolar recovery, bipolar recovery retreats, bipolar athletes, bipolar celebrities, bipolar depression, bipolar mania, bipolar mixed states, bipolar psychosis, bipolar books, bipolar quotes.

I came across valuable observations, and funny ones, too:

You get the pain much more than anyone else. But you see the sunrise more beautiful than anyone else.

Sensitive people . . . don't know any other way to live than by extremes because their emotional thermostat is broken.

I hate being bipolar, it's awesome.

I read everything. (I didn't read medical journals yet. I would do that later.) It was comforting. It made things less scary, sometimes even not scary at all. I found lots of answers to questions I had about my life, especially my childhood, and my depression and suicidal thoughts as a kid.

Bipolar I disorder is marked by severe mood episodes, from mania to depression. Bipolar II disorder is milder, with episodes of mood elevation or hypomania, which alternate with bouts of severe depression. (I'm sure there's nothing "mild" when you're experiencing that.) Cyclothymic disorder is alternating, shorter bouts of hypomania and depression. "Mixed features" means symptoms of opposite mood polarities happening at the same time, while you're manic, hypomanic, or depressed—that is, you can be incredibly energetic, sleepless, and have racing thoughts while also feeling despairing, irritable and suicidal.

How long episodes last and how often they present differs from person to person. If you experience four-plus mood episodes in a twelve-month period, it's called "rapid cycling." (You need to experience particular symptoms for a certain minimum number of days for it to count as an "episode.") Rapid cycling can happen at any time during the illness, though some research shows it may be more common later in the life of the illness. Rapid cycling raises the risk of severe depression and suicide attempts, and is likelier to appear in women than in men. Antidepressants may sometimes be associated with triggering or prolonging rapid cycling, but this is as yet just a theory and still being studied. Some people experience "ultra-rapid" cycling: polarity changes (high to low, or low to high) within a week or even a day, though the short time period means that they may not exhibit the full range of symptoms.

The mania of bipolar may need a trigger, or a series of triggers—alcohol, not enough sleep, too much work, other life stresses . . . or maybe the triggers don't even have to be major at all, as long as the brain chemistry gets tipped just enough.

Bipolar disorder very often has a genetic component. If one parent has it, the child has a roughly 10 percent chance to develop the illness. If both parents have it, the likelihood goes up fourfold.

I learned that bipolar disorder affects nearly six million adult Americans. An estimated 2.6 percent of the population was living with what I had—about 1 in 40. You had a lot better odds of being bipolar than playing football at the major college level. I was blown away to learn that it is the sixth-leading cause of disability in the world. It results in a life span shortened, on average, by about a decade. One in five patients with bipolar disorder completes suicide (not attempts, *completes*). An equal number of men and women develop bipolar illness. It is found in all ages, races, ethnic groups, social classes.

And if you expanded it to the larger category that bipolar belongs to, mental illness, then seventy-five million Americans suffer from a disorder of varying severity.

I learned that people with bipolar are unique, deep, and caring. They live extraordinary lives. There were others like me. Not many athletes or celebrities, but some: former NFL player Charles Haley, actress Catherine Zeta-Jones, singer/actress Demi Lovato, and the late actress/writer Carrie Fisher, to name a few.

Even reading lists of bipolar symptoms was comforting because it was me reading about me (though not every symptom applied):

Mania Episode Signs and Symptoms:

- Increased energy, activity, restlessness
- Euphoric mood
- Extreme irritability
- Poor concentration
- Racing thoughts, fast talking, jumping between ideas
- Sleeplessness
- Heightened sense of self-importance
- Spending sprees
- Increased sexual behavior
- Abuse of drugs, such as cocaine, alcohol and sleeping medications
- Provocative, intrusive or aggressive behavior
- Denial that anything is wrong

Depressive Episode Signs and Symptoms:

- Sad, anxious or empty-feeling mood
- Feelings of hopelessness and pessimism
- Feelings of guilt, worthlessness and helplessness
- Loss of interest or pleasure in activities once enjoyed, including sex
- Decreased energy, fatigue
- Difficulty concentrating, remembering or making decisions
- Restlessness and irritability
- Sleeplessness or sleeping too much
- Change in appetite, unintended weight loss or gain
- Bodily symptoms not caused by physical illness or injury
- Thoughts of death or suicide

Was any of this caused or worsened by my days playing football? I had anxiety as a kid but ultimately it subsided, at least for pockets of time. During my football career, I knocked out a lot of guys—and also had my share of getting my "bell rung." There were quarters of games I could not remember right afterward. Sometimes I didn't feel the biggest hits, while the littlest ones hurt the most. And the particular formation I was often involved in—busting the wedge, on kickoffs—was such a breeding ground for violent injury that the NFL outlawed it a couple years after I retired from the league.

But I don't put it on football. First, I had had childhood depression and thoughts of suicide long before I ever played the sport.

And, as I mentioned, there's a genetic component: The majority of those with bipolar disorder have at least one close relative with the illness. My cousin, it turned out—I learned this after I was diagnosed—had been bipolar but "med non-compliant." A heroin addict, she died of an overdose at age thirty-seven. My Grandpa Howdo, who to me as a young kid had always just seemed shy or maybe antisocial, except for those occasions when he seemed incredibly energetic, the life of the party, suffered from clinical depression, sadly undiagnosed his entire life. Of course, he wasn't alone in having his very serious condition go without being identified or treated. Virtually no one from his generation who suffered from a similar condition got real help, or those from the generation before his, or even the one after, that my parents belonged to.

Now, thankfully, I had the benefit of a diagnosis, and professionals dedicated to helping people like me, and medicine designed to lessen the effect of the worst symptoms . . . yet I was still hesitant to talk about what I had. Who wants the stigma?

Chapter 10

A LIFE OF ITS OWN

Outside of work, I isolated myself from everyone but my inner circle. It took a toll on me because I needed the outlet of people. The isolation was almost as bad as the illness itself. But the depression and anxiety held me back from talking to anyone about it except for my close family and my therapist. I had lived for thirty years without spilling my guts about my innermost thoughts and fears and perpetual anxiety . . . and now I was supposed to tell acquaintances or colleagues all about my diagnosis of mental illness? No, I don't think so. Having been a successful high school athlete and college athlete and then NFL player, my life had always been more public than most. But even if my "dangerous" football personality was on display on a big green field, 120 yards long by 53^1/₃ yards wide, in front of tens of thousands live and millions at home, and even if my brain wiring was partly responsible for making me the player I was, I did not particularly want to turn myself inside out, enough for people from my town or former teammates or strangers to judge, to see what had been inside, ticking, all along.

I chose to live the secret.

In one way, I felt fortunate. Jill and I had been back living in Buffalo for only a little more than a year before I got diagnosed, and so we hadn't had much time to reacquaint with old friends and make new ones. That made it easier to isolate myself than if I had been back for a decade.

Wow. That shows how screwed up my thinking was. *Isn't it great that I can cut myself off from life?*

Maybe for some people a diagnosis is liberating, and they use it to let people in. Not me. Once I was diagnosed, I didn't call anyone. Some friends called but I almost never picked up my phone. Eventually, it stopped ringing. Now and then I would talk on the phone to Ka'aina, in Hawaii, and to Jimmy, my best friend from high school who was now working in Manhattan, but they were both far away. My parents were extremely supportive—when I let them in. They were there for me during the darkest days of my depression. Other times, I felt that they were in total denial about my diagnosis, as if they thought I was overreacting or that I could just snap out of it.

Then again, my judgment of other people's judgment was not exactly state-of-the-art.

Anyway, even if they *were* sometimes in denial, or they thought I had more control, how was that *their* fault? They didn't fully understand the condition, and how could I blame them when *I* didn't fully understand it either?

It had been almost a year since Jill's miscarriage and we had not been able to get pregnant again.

When I wasn't working, I slept. I just stayed in my house, in my living room, and in my bed. Or on the floor in the front hallway, near the sunlight. I gained weight, and my physical health declined along with my mental health.

I did find enough energy to get a tattoo of a bear on my left shoulder and arm. One eye was blue, the other red.

~

Howdo died, at age ninety-five.

I behaved well at my grandfather's funeral in Warren, Pennsylvania—almost too well. I felt detached from my surroundings. That's probably not so odd for funerals, even when it's for a person you were close to or identified with, as I did with Howdo. Funerals are surreal. Even normal people can be surprised by their reactions.

But this felt different. I didn't shed a tear the day of the funeral. Or the day after. Jill asked me about it.

"I don't know if it's the meds or how I felt or because Howdo is now where he wanted to be," I said.

Yet another moment in my life where I had no idea who or what was doing the feeling. And I never would.

~

Sometimes, I felt something bordering on happiness, to think there were people out there who now knew that something was up with me.

But an hour later I could just as easily feel huge regret about having gotten anyone, even my parents, involved in my shit.

Jill was finally beginning to crack. Can you blame her? It was a marvel she hadn't done it sooner. She started seeing a therapist, who recommended she also go to a support group or speak to the women's ministry leader at our church. Jill thought she would do both. I had dumped so much on her, my most trusted friend and partner, and now she needed to vent and be properly heard.

I did not shut everyone out. Maybe the one person I could talk to most honestly through all of this, aside from Jill and my parents and my therapist, was our housepainter.

I met Phil when we hired him to paint our house when we first moved in. When he would take a break from his painting duties, he and I would smoke cigarettes and talk politics or general stuff. His wife, I would later learn, was bipolar, and also suffered from drug addiction. Phil was a great listener. Many people think they're great listeners but they aren't, not really. Phil truly was. He actually responded directly and thoughtfully and totally honestly to what I had just said, no matter the subject we were discussing.

After I got diagnosed, I would sometimes go to Phil's house in the evening and we would sit in his garage, smoking cigarettes and talking about life. There might have been another reason Phil was easy to talk with. Maybe the fact that we didn't know each other that well or for that long made it easier. He didn't know the football side of me, nor did he care. He wasn't interested to see my Super Bowl ring. Maybe our communication worked because we came from different backgrounds. He was always a housepainter and didn't have much. We lived in the same town but while Phil had a small, bungalow-style house, Jill and I lived in the part with big, "nicer" houses. But we clicked. Our conversations were refreshingly frank. On a typical freezing winter night, standing in the driveway, we might go from talking about ice fishing (he talked about that, and I listened) to how much the Buffalo Bills sucked to topics that really mattered. Once, at my place, I remember Phil saying, "Look at you, man. You have all the money in the world, a huge house, a beautiful wife, and you're going through these very hard times and nobody knows."

He took a drag on his cigarette. He gestured at the McMansion outside the window. "Look at that fucking huge house over there. I bet they're dealing with some shit, too. And your next door neighbor? Who *knows* what goes on over there. It doesn't matter who you are, where you live, how much money you have. Behind every closed door, something's going on."

It's how I started to think about America, and mental illness.

Because I was on a cocktail of drugs, I experienced a host of side effects. My insomnia had made me a sleeping man walking for years, but now my fatigue was at a different level. (Or was it "just" the addition of true depression that made it that way?) Once, while driving, I nodded off and hit some construction cones. Fortunately nothing bad happened, not even a scratch on the car, but I realized that I should not be driving at all. Not that I stopped. When I told the psychiatrist that I sometimes fell asleep behind the wheel when driving, she shrugged. It was the meds causing me to fall asleep, she said—but then she did nothing to change the mix.

I needed to drive for my job, so I kept driving.

On another occasion, I fell asleep standing up, in the operating room during a surgery. Another time, right after an operation, a physician's assistant approached me outside the OR and asked if I was okay. One of the surgeons I'd frequently worked with asked me if I was "out partying all night." No, but I *was* in a fog from all the medication and barely able to stay awake.

During conversations, I faded in and out. At a lunch with my boss and a very important surgeon we were hoping to persuade to come on board (i.e., have him agree to use our instruments), the surgeon turned to ask me a question and I realized I had stopped paying attention long ago.

Oh, shit, what were the last words he said and what were we talking about before that . . . ?

The surgeon kept looking at me.

"I'm sorry, can you repeat that?" I asked.

He did, and I stumbled through an answer until my boss took over. After lunch, my boss took me aside. "Keith, you can't do shit like that," he said, totally in the right.

On those rare occasions when Jill and I would go out to dinner with friends, it was 50/50 that at some point I would fall asleep at the table.

Life was fog, with occasional bursts of other weather—some sun, some rain. You don't get a lot of sunshine and all that supposedly helpful vitamin D when you're going through a Buffalo winter. I thought all the time about moving—usually to Arizona but sometimes to California. Why not? As long as it was warm and far away.

The fog persisted. Doctor appointments, medication, changes in medication.

The doctor wanted me to do meditation, yoga, karate.

I tried my relaxation audio. Sometimes, before bed, it actually worked. Sometimes.

Sometimes TV was enjoyable. Sometimes I couldn't sit still enough to watch. I needed to get out and run errands.

I was paranoid about my reputation among those connected to NAU.

I worked, but could barely get out of bed.

I slept too much. Other times I was so agitated that Jill told me to relax all day—"And that's an order!"

Klonopin Ambien Lexapro lazy anxious anxiety anxious manic hypo—

You know what I had to stop doing but just couldn't? These "all or nothing" beliefs. It's not *all* terrible or *all* incredible. It's not just yes or no. You can't live like that. No one can live like that.

If the antidepressant I was taking helped me deal with my down mood but had the "side effect" of pushing me into mania, had I gained something?

Yes.

But other times no.

Or probably, but not as much as I wanted. Because the depressive side was still there, lurking. I didn't want to do anything. I didn't want to work out. I wanted a break from everything.

It looked like Cymbalta would need to be a permanent medication for me, for social anxiety. Or maybe I'd go on Paxil. But Paxil had more side effects, at least for me.

Being on mood stabilizers and antidepressants was like driving a car with one foot on the gas (antidepressants) *and* one foot on the brakes (mood stabilizers).

What if I moved up the time of day I took my meds—would that make a difference?

One doctor said that this was not a medicine problem. I needed to develop good habits, a routine. Build a healthier foundation to fight my illness. Medication is vital . . . but it can only do so much.

At a sales meeting in Fort Lauderdale, I was anxious about not drinking because everyone drinks when they're there. They would expect me to drink. It would be strange if I didn't. Throughout the socializing parts, I felt uncomfortable. I had nothing to say. I was certain that people noticed that I was incapable of carrying on a conversation. So I had half a beer to loosen up. That didn't help, so I left the party early.

The next day, we had presentations to make. We were in groups of five and I was the one chosen to do our presentation. (Because I'm a people person!) I was sure I flubbed it. I was sure that people noticed. Immediately afterward, I called Jill, upset, wanting to come home early from the conference. She calmed me down, told me to take my Klonopin, do some deep breathing, and tell my bosses about the situation.

I did. I told my superiors. They were understanding and supportive. One of them told me I could leave the conference early.

Once I was home, of course, I grew massively disappointed in myself.

I needed a different career. No way I could be a full-time sales rep.

The next day was a new day—or was it hypomania? I went to church, did yoga, ran errands, went to my parents' for dinner.

Fog descends.

At the psychiatrist's urging, Jill started keeping a mood chart for me.

I wanted us to move to California. I would work in a bar, Jill would do nursing, we'd live in a small apartment on the beach, we'd spend our days running on the beach, living life, live an adventurous life.

I thought we should move to Arizona.

We couldn't move to Arizona (or California) because of my family. They needed me. I needed them. We needed them. Someone needed someone.

I couldn't do another winter like this, which is like every Buffalo winter.

I had trouble making decisions. Sometimes I wanted Jill to make all the decisions.

I worried so much about the future. Jill kept reminding me to stay in the present.

But wait, I didn't know which was which. When I told my boss more details of what I had been through and how I wanted to stay an associate sales rep for now and not move up to senior rep because I did not feel capable of taking on more responsibility, wasn't that me living in the present? Or was that unacceptable because you always had to be planning the next step? Up, up, up? And wasn't there something really fucked-up about that? Wasn't that how pretty much everyone lived in America, including most "normal" people—focused always on the next step, the future, not grounded in the present?

But I also dwelled in the past. I could have been better at football. I could have had a better career.

I was bored.

I didn't know if I was depressed or unhappy.

I hated my job. I tried to deal with it by not caring about it, which worked as a strategy until I came up with another reason to remember to hate it.

I couldn't live with the decisions I'd made.

Often I just wanted it to be the two of us, just Jill and me. Fog.

Then, after six months of this, the hiding and hibernating, things . . . lifted. Well, I don't know if "lifted" is the right word. I was no longer staggering in the deepest, darkest depths of depression, and for that I was incredibly grateful. But now that depression was replaced by an epic new level of anxiety—one I did not know existed. Because that was slightly better than the paralysis of the depression, I became at least a little more normal-seeming. I started to go more frequently to my parents' house, a 20-minute drive, and I'd just talk to them. I would often ask my dad to get in the hot tub with me so we could just sit there and talk. I needed someone to vent to other than my therapist and Jill and Phil. When I was growing up, Dad was gone much of the time because of the demands of the coaching life. But now, at age thirty, I needed him most, and luckily he was there. I can't exactly say why I was drawn to him over other family members. Maybe it was his calm demeanor. Maybe, like Phil, he just had a genuine gift for listening. He seemed to have all the right responses. He never judged. And when he gave his opinion, it was well thought out.

Meanwhile, Jill had started attending meetings of the National Alliance on Mental Illness (NAMI) to better understand bipolar disorder and mental illness. Some of it was good for her—she got to see many other people who were in her situation. *Our* situation. But it was equally scary for her—she got to see what life could be like for her, for us, fifteen years down the road, if things got worse, if I became med noncompliant.

If a child of ours had bipolar.

It was at a NAMI meeting where someone suggested to her that it might help me to attend a bipolar support group.

When she returned home from the meeting and told me about the idea, I didn't want to.

I was too lethargic to agree to do anything or go anywhere, even things that might help.

~

Believe it or not, I was offered a promotion at work. If it wasn't so unfunny, it would have been funny: me, right then, making the corporate jump. As an associate rep, you put in your time until they're ready to kick you up to senior rep—in essence, your boss's position. My boss knew I didn't want the position, nor could I handle it, but he emailed me anyway to offer it. It was somewhat amusing that he emailed me the offer rather than just asking me, but they probably needed it in writing.

I emailed back: "Thank you for the opportunity, but at this time I don't think this position is suited for me."

Once I had turned down the promotion, the company hired someone from outside who would be my new boss. It was up to me to train him, which was too much to handle. I called my old boss, asked him to meet me at the local Panera, and told him there that I was resigning. Medical device sales was no longer for me. I needed a clean start.

Then again, resigning your job without any idea what employment is out there, combined with a mental illness diagnosis, combined with a feeling that you're stuck in your house and you're highly antisocial . . . that does not make things easier. It actually makes you feel overwhelmed by life, times ten. Without a job or structured purpose, the veil of depression and the constant jackhammer of anxiety on my brain confined me to my home even more.

And just around that time, what do you know? Jill got pregnant again.

~

Kevin had a Super Bowl–viewing party at his house in nearby Wheatfield. I shouldn't have gone. I didn't feel like talking or even just looking happy. Mostly the funk was because of how down I generally felt, but also because I was now obsessing over how much better I could have been at football. I started playing the deadly "What If?" game. Time and again Jill had reminded me not to. After all, she said, you can *always* look at things in different ways. You can always be sad about what you didn't achieve so why not be happy about all that you *did* achieve? You *did* play in the Super Bowl. You won. You did well.

And once you start the "What If?" game, it's hard to stop.

I regretted spending so much of my money. What if I hadn't?

I regretted our big house. What if we had chosen to live life in a smaller home, with less stuff, out in the country? Maybe we would have been happier there.

"What if" was the manic side of me, exploring every single option.

What if I drove my car off the road, so it could all be over?

What if my airbag didn't work?

I didn't want to commit suicide but I *did* wish, at least sometimes, that something would happen to me and I would die.

I eventually shared my suicidal thoughts with Jill—not all the times I had them, but some of the time. She did exactly what our therapist and her support group advised her to do. First, she would ask me if I had a plan. I always said no, of course, but I did have one. Maybe it was a plan I didn't intend to follow through on, but it was a plan. I wanted to overdose because that would be the most peaceful way to do it; just fall asleep, right?

She asked me how often I had these thoughts. About twice a week, I told her, though it was more than that.

Most of the time she would just let me talk, vent. She was a great listener and would respond with, "So many people love you. We're going to get through this, you're going to get through this. It's okay. You have me. I'm not going anywhere."

Once, I said to Jill, "I'm glad I don't own a gun because it would be tempting."

"Would you ever buy one?" she asked.

"No," I said.

~

A vacuum of meaning. Maybe meaning and purpose would automatically appear with the birth of our child. For now, nothing. Something needed to fill that vacuum. Even when awake I was useless. I had twin liabilities: My impulsiveness kept me from following any sort of plan consistently while my overthinking prevented me from formulating one I could follow to begin with.

I became obsessed with death and the afterlife and began intensely studying near-death experiences. I read about them for weeks.

Jill had already lost so much by the time I was diagnosed with bipolar. Now, a year into this new phase, she planned to quit her job to take care of me.

And she was pregnant with our first child.

~

Even when you can't control something, like depression, like bipolar, even when your loved ones appreciate that it's not something you want to do, to yourself or to them, you still can't help but feel awful about the effect it's having on them—that is, when you're not too busy thinking and worrying about your own pain, which is most of the time. Given what Jill had been through to keep me afloat, to keep us afloat, to go to all my meetings with me, to make sure I was taking my meds, to work part-time as a nurse to keep us going financially—it won't come as a surprise that now *she* was diagnosed with depression. They called it "situational depression" because it was very much connected with life circumstances, not because of something purely chemical.

The pressure on her for years, day by day, was immense. She had to walk this fine line which I suppose everyone living with a mentally unstable person has to do. When talking to me, when listening to me, when taking care of me, she was trying to be reasonable and responsible—but was taking it easy on me the right thing? When did she need to push me, so that I would get out of bed, or stop taking her for granted, or stop acting like The Bear? And when would pushing me hard turn into pushing me *too* hard?

She needed time off—time off from me, really, but that wasn't going to happen anytime soon. At the least, she needed time off from work. She needed taking care of. She had spent a decade on a rollercoaster ride with me and my illness, me undiagnosed and then me diagnosed, and now she needed a break. Her whole life had become about taking care of me. She was planning her every day around my needs. "The sickest member in a family is often *not* the identified patient," one of my many doctors had once said—and while there was no way that anyone in the family was taking the top prize from me, that didn't mean that Jill did not need treatment and caring, too. I just wasn't capable of giving it to her.

~

In early 2012, I changed to new medications, again, without all that much improvement. And so many of them at once! Severe anxiety was my new default. It seemed as if for each percentage my depression went down, my anxiety went up, which was depressing in itself because I realized I would always have some set amount of mental illness in me. It could only ever be shifted, not eliminated. I wasn't paranoid anymore about my mind or phones being tapped, yet contemplating and dealing with real life was proving to be as tough as dealing with an alternate, paranoid reality version of life. I could think more clearly about what was going on but what confronted me filled me with anxiety. With so many medications, I no longer knew if what I felt was illness, the medicine, or both. I was seeing a psychiatrist once every six weeks to discuss medication for fifteen minutes, and a therapist once every other week. Yet, despite the regular contact with doctors, I still experienced anxiety, depressive states, irritability, obsessive thoughts, and suicidal ideation.

And yet things had been worse. I knew that. And because of Jill's situation, I felt I owed it to both of us to finally attend one of those bipolar support meetings she had told me about.

~

Here's something weird: Before I went to a support meeting for those suffering with bipolar, I had never met someone who *clearly* had it.

The meeting was held in the basement of an old brick building in downtown Buffalo. I didn't know what to expect so I didn't say much. I would estimate there were fifteen people. A lawyer, a psychiatric nurse, a teacher, a landscaper, a software engineer, a clerk, a bunch of others. More than one person who was out of work. More than one on disability. We sat in a circle, like I imagined. We had to introduce ourselves.

"Hi, I'm Keith. I was diagnosed a year and a half ago," I said when it came my turn in the circle. "It's been hard. This is my first session, I'm just going to listen tonight, thanks." That was it out of me.

As the hood on my hoodie went up, I studied each person carefully.

Am I really like these people? Am I as bad as this guy? That lady over there gives me anxiety when she speaks—why? That guy's a lawyer, for Christ sake, why is he here? Wait, why am I here? What am I going to say?

As I listened to stories of struggle and recovery, the first conclusion I came to: *There are people out there in worse shape than I am.*

I couldn't help but be grateful for my loving wife, the fact that Jill had stood by my side through everything, and be grateful for the baby she was carrying. I had an amazing supportive family and great friends. Thanks to the NFL, I had good health insurance. Now, I could tell myself that I wasn't alone.

As the session continued and everyone shared their stories I began to get emotional. There were moments about love, reconciliation, music that brought hope, pets being emotional lifesavers, real steps toward wellness . . . but that was not what I was drawn to. Those anecdotes disappeared into the stale air in the room as soon as people recounted them. No, I was drawn to the dark side of the conversation—the struggle. Stories of medication complications. Divorce. Hopelessness. Anxiety. Homelessness. Abuse. Custody battles. Loneliness. Malpractice. Hospital stays.

It was an eerie feeling I had as I sat there, listening and watching. More than eerie, it was . . . satisfying? Is that what I felt? I truly understood their pain. For the first time in my life, I was among others like me. It was the first time I had met someone else with bipolar disorder speak intimately about it—and I was getting it all at once, in all shapes and sizes and colors.

It was like knowing a language, a language that only you speak—and then the first time you meet others who know the language, they don't just know it but they speak it fluently, as well as you ever could, and they don't slow down to explain this verb or noun or these vocabulary words, they just talk. And talk. And you understand everything they're saying. Including things that you feared saying aloud.

After thirty minutes of stories, I felt a pit in my stomach. The only thought I had was: *When can I leave?* Things were getting too real. Every time I made eye contact with someone I felt embarrassment: I saw myself in the eyes and voices and stories of these strangers. Did it matter that some were in far worse condition? No. And, anyway, some seemed way *ahead* of me. Worse, better—it almost didn't matter. We were all bonded.

I could stand to go to only three or four such meetings. They brought me down instead of lifted me up. One woman—definitely manic, definitely paranoid— just couldn't stop talking. She went on and on about how she lived in her parents' basement and couldn't even see a doctor because her health insurance didn't cover it. She said she was forty years old and complained that she was too old to be living with her parents. She complained that she couldn't exercise because her ankle hurt. In a room full of stressed-out people, she stressed us all out more (I believe)—certainly me.

There was a landscaper who always sat next to me. He was pretty cool. He rode his bike to the sessions because of multiple DUIs. But there, too, the struggle far outshone the recovery. He was going through an ugly divorce and custody battle, and it was made worse because he seemed—to me, anyway—pretty healthy and with it. I felt bad for him.

The psychiatric nurse seemed one hundred percent normal. People said he never missed a meeting and had been coming to them for years. He was the veteran of the group, the one participant everyone else looked up to. He rarely spoke but when he did, people listened extra carefully. He mostly talked about the difficulty, the challenge, of balancing his high-stress job and his illness.

I knew that support groups helped many people, but I was not one of them. And it wasn't because it reminded me of what I was going through. It was because it reminded me what a truly silent epidemic this was—bipolar, mental illness, mental illness in America. (I didn't know that it was better or worse in the rest of the world.) Here we were, fifteen strangers, gathering once a week, at a not particularly convenient time, sitting in the basement of some nothing office building, depressing grey walls, folding metal chairs, lukewarm coffee, here to talk about the thing that absolutely defined us as much as anything, more than almost anything. These were people with wives, husbands, partners, children, parents, siblings, friends, coworkers, careers, mortgages, backyards, cats and dogs. And most of the rest of the people in the world, including many of the loved ones of those people, didn't understand what was going on, what the condition really felt like, or they were simply uncomfortable talking about it.

And there I was, sitting in my chair, the ex-linebacker, Super Bowl champion, thinking about the people with mental illness who, like me, were lucky enough to have in their lives people they loved and who loved them. Yet so many people with mental illness live alone, either because they can't be with others or maybe others can't be with them. Or both.

In basements across the country, I thought, such people were sitting in circles talking about their struggles with mental illness, and most likely it was the one time in the week they talked about it out loud, where the point was that someone else would hear it.

I stopped going. I kept quiet.

~

Why was this happening to me, to Jill, to us? How had bipolar picked me, which then seeped out to affect everyone around me that I cared about? Why was my brain chemistry the way it was, enabling this to happen? One theory suggests that bipolar disorder is caused by, or related to, abnormal serotonin chemistry in the brain. Serotonin is a neurotransmitter that affects mood, because it affects so many things that influence mood—sleep, wakefulness, eating, sexual activity, impulsiveness, learning, and memory. So if something's off with your serotonin, it could cause mood swings. The level or functioning of two other brain chemicals, noradrenaline (norepinephrine) and dopamine, may also have an effect. Noradrenaline (as well as serotonin) has been linked to depression and bipolar disorder. Dopamine regulates circuitry in the brain areas that control pleasure and emotional reward. Disruption of these circuits seems to be linked to psychosis and schizophrenia.

Whatever was happening in there had very real, day-to-day effects on who and how I was.

I felt invisible in social settings. If not invisible, then I was at least not present. When I was with people, including kids, I didn't give anything to them. I let others do all the work.

I needed a change. I needed a job. I hired a career counselor to help me work on my interview skills. I called a headhunter.

Maybe I didn't want to go into the business world. *You know what? I would make a great teacher*, I thought. I would have to start as a part-time substitute teacher. There might even be an opening at my old high school, Sweet Home. I could even do lawn work for extra money. We could use it.

I wanted to get better. That was always the goal.

I felt so tired.

I felt so tired of feeling tired.

I felt so tired of feeling tired of feeling tired.

There was a party at Chuck E. Cheese for my nephews. The whole time I was there, which wasn't all that long, I could not muster a smile. Jill had to socialize for the both of us. In the car ride home, I talked with her for the millionth time (for me it didn't seem like nearly that much, for Jill it probably felt like the billionth) about how down I was. "I hope heaven is better than this," I said. When we got home, I went over to Phil's for a smoke. The next morning, I went to church. Sometimes it helped. Sometimes it didn't.

Jill's patience was running thin. Her nerves, her emotions. This was so unfair to her.

~

On April 27, 2012, our son, Connor Douglas O'Neil, was born. It was the most beautiful, incredible experience of my life. Could it be a turning point? The beginning of the end of the struggle?

In a sense, yes. But not the way you would ever want it to play out.

"You never know," my father had told me, when he encouraged me to stick it out the beginning of junior year of college, when I was all set to transfer because I had been passed over for a starting slot. And then the guy in front of me breaks his leg.

"You never know," the Dallas Cowboys scout told me, after he spotted me at a game, even though he wasn't supposed to be there, even though he was there to scout a player on the other team. And that's how I ended up in the league.

Your beautiful, amazing wife gives birth to a beautiful, amazing boy—a miracle to begin with, even more so when you consider the miscarriage she went through, followed by a year of not getting pregnant—and you figure it's got to be the best thing that ever happened to you, right?

You never know.

Chapter 11

HOW DO YOU EVEN KNOW YOUR NAME?

Some dates in a family's life stand out more than others. For the O'Neils, August 26 is a big one—my birthday, the date that both my father's and my NFL careers essentially ended, the date that Jill and I announced she was pregnant for the first time. August 26 is a red-letter day for us, some good, some not so good.

Then there's July 6.

Connor was ten weeks old.

For the previous year and a half, I had been on a ton of different medications. I had been unemployed for months. I would lie in bed all day, often thinking about dying.

I had told my therapist that I had suicidal thoughts. I had told the psychiatrist, and Jill. But for all my frankness with doctors, I talked about it very seldom with them, as if it was an afterthought. *Nothing to see here. Let's move on to the REAL problem. Just ignore any mention of killing myself, thanks.*

Why did I not talk more about it with them, when they were professionals who dealt with this kind of thing?

I can give you excuses—I didn't want to scare them too much; it's a no-turning-back sort of conversation.

How dumb of me.

With Jill, it was different. I now told her everything. I knew I had to. At one point, during another bout of depression and hopelessness, I got vague in a way that is actually not vague at all. She knew what I was thinking about.

"Do you have plans?" she asked.

"I've thought about just taking a bunch of pills," I said.

"Would you do it?"

"No, I wouldn't."

"Why didn't you tell the doctor?"

"I don't know."

Later, she told me that she planned on hiding all my pills, for my safety.

Then . . . time passed. I was on the upswing, having figured out that I really wanted to be a teacher. (It was just another of my many fleeting thoughts. Who knew how serious?)

So I kept it mostly to myself.

The night of July 6, 2012, I had been contemplating going back to school to get a teaching degree in special education. The school semester had already started, as had the class I wanted to take. That night, I was planning to email an academic advisor at the school to see if she would still let me enroll.

At some point, Jill innocently asked me if I had followed through with the advisor. It was a totally legitimate question, given how important I had been saying it was to me to become a teacher, and given how distracted I could get.

No, I told her.

"I can't keep on top of everything," she said. "You have to be responsible for your own life."

What she said upset me. I somehow convinced myself that she had yelled it, though another part of me knew that she hadn't. But that part of me, the more reasonable part, was usually the one not getting a vote on how I experienced reality and expressed myself.

I went upstairs and lay in bed. Again, my mind was flooded with thoughts of suicide. I wanted to die. I wanted it to end.

It. Everything.

I went downstairs to talk to Jill again. I sat down on the couch with her. I told her I was feeling very suicidal. Throughout our conversation she was calm and collected. She asked me the questions. *Do you have a plan?* There were other questions I could list here but that would not be truthful because I did not remember her asking them or, probably more truthfully, I did not remember hearing them.

Whatever was said, the conversation was brief. Or it *seemed* brief. She herself was tired, worn down by my illness. Wow, if that's not an understatement.

Oh, yes: And she—we—she also had a ten-week-old baby to look after. Connor was not an afterthought for her, as he sometimes was, at that moment in my life, for me. After

Connor was born, I got his name tattooed over my heart. But it was just a tattoo. I was still consumed by how I felt.

A few minutes went by. Or seconds. Jill and I began arguing about something else, something stupid. The fight ended.

I decided to kill myself.

Back upstairs, I looked in the mirror, trying to decide if I wanted to do it right then or wait until after something else.

I talked to my mother on the phone, a pretty normal conversation. I didn't say anything about my plan.

I paced back and forth for minutes, no idea how many. Terrible as it is to admit, I was not at all thinking of Jill or Connor. I did not think about the effect that finding me in our bed would have on my wife or, years later, my son. I did not think to write a note.

In the bathroom, I opened the medicine cabinet and counted out my Ambien pills: 49. For some reason I remember the exact number. I paced back and forth.

I emptied the contents of the bottle down my throat.

I went back into the bedroom. I lay on the bed for what seemed like an hour. It was probably just a few minutes, if that. Then it hit me: I'm going to die soon.

What had I done?

I knew Jill was downstairs. She was probably washing baby bottles and waiting the half-hour or so until Connor woke in his swing to be fed and put to bed.

I began to fade. I was fading. I picked up my phone. Somehow I got to the text screen. I got to Jill's name. I texted *need to go to the hospital*

The rest of what I recall from July 6 is mostly fragments.

Jill, there, asking me what I had done, how many pills I had taken.

She slapped me a few times.

She yelled at me to stay awake.

Dialed 911.

That's the last I remember of July 6.

~

I remember being wheeled on a gurney into BryLin Hospital, a psychiatric facility in Buffalo. It was the next day, July 7.

The previous night (I was told) I had spent under medical supervision in the psychiatric unit of Erie County Medical Center. Strangely, I had been fairly alert and even able to walk, though I occasionally stumbled.

I came to at about one o'clock the next afternoon, as they wheeled me into BryLin on a stretcher. I had slept for sixteen hours. My wife and parents were by my side. I remember this part a bit, even with some remaining portion of the 49 Ambien pills still in my system. I was checked in (I don't remember that part). I was asked to remove my clothing down to my underwear. I put on other clothes that someone had brought. I was wearing my Cowboys mesh shorts. Nothing in my clothes could include drawstrings, shoelaces, belts, anything I could use to harm myself. I was brought to a room. A man was sleeping in the other bed, though he was so still I didn't notice him at first. Jill and my parents were asked to leave. I was on my own, alone. I recall sitting on the edge of my bed, enclosed by white walls, wondering how long I would be there. And as I sat there, things became gradually clearer. I was there because I had tried to kill myself. This is where I was.

I must have fallen asleep because the next thing I remember was waking up. It was dark outside and tears were rolling down the sides of my face. My heart was racing. Flat pillow, tiny blanket, as bad as on an airplane—but this was a hospital! For sick, crazy people! Could they not provide a little more comfort?

Wedges of light fanned out across the ceiling. The light originated from outside, shining up from the street and scattering through the blinds shielding the window. The door to my room was opened a crack, letting in another slice of light.

Is this where my life has taken me? What happened to my life? Where did it go? I was once somebody. Is this real? Am I even alive anymore?

That first night I hardly thought of my family at all. I was too numb and confused and in my own head to fully grasp what I had done and how it would affect everyone who loved me. I had a beautiful wife and a two-month-old baby boy at home whom I had just tried to leave, forever. I had a mother, a father, a brother, a sister, along with eight nieces and nephews whom I had attempted to leave forever. And I felt no remorse. Because I was sick. Thoughts of death still filled my mind. I was stuck in a bipolar episode. I was manic, depressed, anxious, and scared, with a mind still consumed by thoughts of suicide. This new psychiatric facility was exactly where I belonged.

I fought to fall back asleep but what felt almost like electricity was passing through my body, in bursts. Was it the Ambien, or general anxiety? The periodic shocks were something I had never experienced before. They traveled from my feet through to my head. Was it just some bizarre sort of identification with what I had learned earlier that day—that my "roommate" had been getting ECT, or electroconvulsive therapy, which was sometimes used on those with major depression when medication wasn't working? Now he was sleeping so silently and still, I truly thought he was dead.

Should I tell someone? I would not see him awake for one minute of the seven days I spent at BryLin.

I awoke the following morning in a foreign place. The first few seconds of wakefulness were so peaceful because I had forgotten where I was and why. It was the last moment of peace I experienced that day. Reality set in, anxiety, symptoms. Fatigue, because I could not have slept for more than four hours. My chest felt like it was going to explode. I began pacing. I was sweating. I again contemplated suicide. The single positive thought was that the hospital-appointed psychiatrist was coming around that afternoon.

It was first-come, first-serve for the one psychiatrist who was showing up, so I hurried to get in line. On my way there, I passed a room that was being turned over. They were hosing down the mattress. I asked someone about it and she said that when a patient leaves, they not only cleaned the sheets but steam-cleaned them. It made me feel like we were animals.

As I positioned myself to see the psychiatrist, I was eager to speak with someone about my current state. A stranger, all the better. The doctor finally arrived wearing what looked like a suit three sizes too big and carrying a large stack of folders. He walked into a room—not an office, just a room—and plopped his files down on a chair. After a couple minutes, he welcomed me. The instant I sat down, I turned angry—not at him but at my current psychiatrist and all the meds she had me on. I had to vent. After a few minutes of this, I started to weep. Then I got hold of myself, sort of, and said, "I need help. Help me. I tried to kill myself. I want this to end, all of it, everything, please help."

The doctor comforted me with his manner as much as his words. He was calm and sincere, not the "all business" approach of my current psychiatrist, who talked only about medication. This doctor talked about medication but also about life. He peppered his conversation with quotations, and even though they were a bit cliché and corny, in the state I was in they were appreciated. "Realize that adversity makes you stronger," he said. "Always laugh and be able to laugh at yourself. Humor is healing . . . Be content with what you have . . . Be thankful for your health in general. It's a blessing to have all five senses and no physical disabilities."

His overall message was right: *It could be worse.*

I liked him a lot—until we began talking about my medication plan. He believed I needed to stay on some medications, eliminate others, and add some new ones, including one that I knew was heavy duty: Trazodone, an antidepressant used for depression and anxiety. I told him that I felt that being on the wrong medication had been partly responsible for my suicide attempt.

But I complied. I would switch to his medication cocktail.

The second night was as bad as the first. I lay in bed hour after hour with only my thoughts and a Bible. Every time I was about to drift off to sleep, the sound of the door opening would startle me. Bed check was every fifteen minutes, as the nurse came around to see that none of us were harming ourselves or each other. The drip-drip-drip of the door opening was driving me insane. I resolved to get out of BryLin as soon as I could. Though it was the middle of the night, I needed to talk to someone. I got out of bed, slowly opened the evil door, and stuck my head out. The hall was dark, silent, empty. Of the few ceiling lights on, a few flickered. I saw no signs of humanity.

I walked down the hall. In the darkened "community room," the TV was on, stuck on the fuzzy channel. *You are definitely in the loony bin now!* I edged further down the hall until I noticed a nurse, up a ways on my right, sitting behind the desk, reading a book by the light of a tiny desk lamp. I approached her.

"Hi, I'm Keith," I said. "I need some medicine to put me to sleep."

"You'll have to wait to see the doctor," she said. "I don't have the power to give you anything right now."

"I need to speak with someone. I think I'm going crazy."

She put down her book and made real eye contact. "You can talk with me if you want."

I don't remember what we talked about but it went on for maybe fifteen minutes. Her demeanor comforted me. I said goodbye and made my way back to my room. I did not sleep the rest of the night.

The next day, during visiting hours, Jill and my parents witnessed my anxiety and the effects of sleep deprivation take over. Head spinning, heart pounding, body shaking, again the feeling as if I was crawling out of my skin. It was not a panic attack but something else, though I did not know what. We were in the community room and I was sitting in an old wooden chair when suddenly, as if something inside my body forced me to do this, I jumped up from the chair and rushed to a stationary bicycle in the corner of the room and sat down on it. For no reason. I just had to move. I was so uncomfortable in my body. Sitting and fidgeting on the bike, I locked eyes with my father. I could see the concerned look in his eyes.

"Get the nurse *now*," I ordered him, in an unusually stern voice. And then I simply had to return to the wooden chair. I was moments away from an explosive anxiety attack, I could tell.

The nurse arrived shortly and took my vitals, as Jill and my parents looked on. My blood pressure was through the roof. "I'm freaking out, my heart is beating through my chest, I haven't slept in a while, I feel like I'm going insane, help me," I said to the nurse. She reassured me that they would take care of me and help me get through this. An IV stand was wheeled in. She hooked my arm up to a drip of the medication Inderal, which is often prescribed to treat such conditions as tremors, angina, and hypertension. At some point my parents left. Jill remained. It wasn't long before the effects of the drug kicked in. I felt warm and comfortable. Finally, everything was peaceful. I started to appreciate my wife's company. It was nice having her there with me, alone, by my side. We were on the floor now. She sat with her back against the wall, and I laid my head in her lap, my body sprawled out on the floor. I had not felt such peace in a very long time. I drifted off to sleep.

That night I woke at around two in the morning. I could not remember Jill leaving or me being put to bed. I was not on the IV drip anymore but I felt better, both mentally and physically. I sat up, sat on the edge of my bed, and looked at my roommate sleeping. He had not moved a muscle since I had arrived. I had stopped worrying about him but was still curious. What pain was he going through that he needed to get shocked like that? I thought of all the people who had passed through that room, occupying my bed and my roommate's bed. Who were they? What was their story? How many had as much trouble sleeping as I did? A lot, probably. How many were still alive? Those that were—what were they doing with their lives?

And that was just one room in the hospital.

I stood to use the bathroom—and my roommate rolled over and spoke gibberish. *Alive!* At least that. In the bathroom mirror, I did not recognize the reflection. I rested my hands on the edge of the sink for support and kept staring in the mirror. Bloodshot eyes, massive purple bags under them, pale skin, bloated face from all the medication. I had put on a lot of weight, roughly fifty pounds, since being diagnosed a year and a half earlier. A far cry from what a professional athlete looks like. If you wanted to see what someone who is "washed up" looked like, this was a pretty good picture.

But that was an evaluation of the physical. What troubled me most was that I did not recognize the person in the mirror. He had no soul. He was lifeless.

There were few things to occupy my mind during the rest of my stay at BryLin. We were offered once-daily group therapy, which after the first session I avoided: Almost nobody came and they were worthless anyway.

At one point, one of the nurses asked, "Are you the Keith O'Neil who used to be on the Dallas Cowboys?" I said yes. She was a huge Cowboys fan. I felt horrible.

The only thing I looked forward to was visiting hours, when my family would come, even though it was tough for me, and tough for them, too.

The remainder of the week—more long days, more sleepless nights—I did not try to befriend a single patient. I did not say a word to another patient. I sat alone with my thoughts and emotions. One of the thoughts: *There has to be one sickest, lowest point in your life—please let these days be it.* Suicidal, unemployed, desperate, and plagued by an illness that had taken full control of my mind and life. I was not spiraling into a dark hole—I was deep in the hole. I felt as if I had nothing—no, not that I *had* nothing, but that there was nothing to hold onto, as I floated through a sea of nothingness . . . no, that's also not it. It's a feeling I can't define. Not with words. I know this: The only feeling I had was of wanting to end it all.

But hold on.

Because the next thought I remember having is the kind of thing that someone who really wants to *live* would have, not someone who just tried to end things: I prayed for purpose. I felt as if I was thirsting for it and my illness was finding any way it could to deprive me of it.

I wanted to be well again. I wanted the hospital stay to be over, all the medications, my illness, the struggle . . . I wanted *them* to be over, not my life. I did not want to discard my life along with all that other stuff. My old life had good things in it.

I was released a week later. My parents, through contacts, were able to set up an appointment for Jill and me with Dr. Steven Dubovsky, Chair and Professor of the Department of Psychiatry at the University at Buffalo.

For my evaluation with Dr. Dubovsky, his office asked us to provide a list of the drugs I had been on over the previous few years. In no particular order:

Geodon (anti-psychotic)
Seroquel (anti-psychotic)
Abilify (anti-psychotic)
Depakote (mood stabilizer)
Trileptal (mood stabilizer)
Lamictal (mood stabilizer, antidepressant)
Cymbalta (antidepressant)
Lexapro (antidepressant)
Wellbutrin XL (antidepressant)

Klonopin (anti-anxiety)

Ativan (anti-anxiety)

Valium (anti-anxiety)

Xanax (anti-anxiety)

Trazodone (anti-anxiety, antidepressant, insomnia)

Ambien (insomnia)

Restoril (insomnia)

In his office, Dr. Dubovsky studied the list, then looked up at me and Jill, sitting across from his desk. He made a curious smile.

"How do you even know your name?" he asked me.

I shrugged. His comment was a compliment, a warning, and a genuinely curious inquiry all in one.

"I don't know," I said. "Can you please help?"

~

Throughout my year and a half of severe depression and anxiety, I felt as if my brother acted as if nothing was happening. I think it was his way of trying to make me feel normal. Kevin didn't seem to understand how I could sleep until one o'clock. To him, it was something I could stop doing if I tried, just tried harder. There was no, *How are you doing?* to specifically address my circumstances. He wouldn't come to me. I had to go to him—but I didn't want to do that, either. I did not want his sympathy. Occasionally I would talk *around* it with him, and he would listen carefully and give feedback, very practical feedback, though it didn't really acknowledge the huge part of bipolar that defies behaving practically. Most of the time he would try to be funny—that's Kevin—trying to lift up his kid brother, but he would never explicitly talk about my illness. It would be about everyday things—his family, his job, my job (eventually my former job), stuff like that. We had been in the same industry and he had always tried to give me good advice. We just never talked about . . . *it*.

That was his way, and many people's way, of keeping it *seeming* more normal: Talk about everyday things, not the abnormality in the room.

Even the suicide attempt didn't get much more than that. We eventually had an enormous argument that somehow grew out of our talking about what I had done, but it was loud and seemed off topic and not really helpful.

I didn't blame Kevin. How could I? He was my idol growing up and I never had a moment where I saw a reason to not feel that way. From childhood until my diagnosis we were as tight as two brothers could be. I could go to him with almost anything. Everyone said we talked alike and walked alike and pretty much carried ourselves the same way. We both worked hard at whatever we did. But there were differences. He was a Type A, me a Type B. He was the life of the party, I was The Bear. He was smarter than I was. He was a very successful medical device sales rep.

My sister was angry about the suicide attempt. Everyone copes differently. After Colleen expressed her anger to me about it, we didn't talk for a month and a half. Then, when we did, we had a blowup about everything. We were very close from childhood through most of college, a relationship that got less close after I met Jill. Colleen had been the one I went to with all my problems. She was the one I vented to when I wasn't getting recruited in high school by any Division I-A colleges. When I was homesick at NAU, I usually called Colleen. When I got arrested, my call from jail was to

Colleen. Then I met Jill, and I didn't "need" Colleen's support the way I once did.

It was tough on me to have my siblings struggling with how to help me. But it was obviously tough on them, too. Up until the attempt, it was hard for them to comprehend that I was so sick, even though I had been going to therapy for a while, to a shrink for over a year, and was on a bunch of medications. I was their baby brother!

One of my doctors once said, "A pathologic family is a tyranny ruled by its sickest member."

No one, not even my brother and sister, knew exactly how to act toward me. There was no playbook.

Jill bought me a wooden plaque to keep next to my side of the bed. The scripture engraved on it read, "'For I know the plans I have for you,' declares the Lord, 'plans to prosper you and not to harm you, plans to give you hope and a future'" (Jeremiah 29:11).

I am not overly religious. But when you are utterly lost, when you're at rock bottom, some sentiments get to you more than others.

I scoured the Internet for wisdom, for self-help books. I came across a memoir, *Save Me from Myself*, by Brian "Head" Welch, lead guitarist of Korn. He talked about how he kicked drugs and found God. I read it in two days. In the book, I came across another scripture: "'Come to me all who are weary and burdened and I will give you rest'" (Matthew 11:28). I found myself reading the Bible. Before I knew it, I had finished almost the entire New Testament. I needed something, anything, to get me through the darkest, hardest days of my life.

I realized that suicide doesn't end the pain. It just passes it on to others.

~

Regardless of the support that was or wasn't there—or was there but in a complicated way—I found myself months later in a much different place. Some things people can do better than anything else. Sometimes medication is unbeatable.

To my plea to Dr. Dubovsky—"Can you please help?"—the doctor absolutely delivered. He found me a new psychiatrist. We began the arduous, months-long process of changing all my medications. We settled on a new, much simpler regimen. By early 2013, he had weaned me off of all three antidepressants and had me on only one mood stabilizer, lithium—in his words, the "gold standard" medication for bipolar disorder. When I asked him why my previous psychiatrists had not thought to start me off with lithium, he said, "Some of these young doctors like all the new, sexy drugs."

Within six months of that initial meeting with him, I was a different person. I was out of the fog caused by my illness and the barrage of previous medications. I actually felt a renewed desire to move my body. My mind began to think again. I was living again.

Almost everyone in the bipolar community has medication stories to share. Each individual must go through the grueling process of finding a combination of drugs that works for him or her. And it's an individual process. For some, it's easier than others. Just because one medication worked for me didn't mean it was going to work for someone else. I found this fact about the human brain fascinating.

Still, even though things were looking up and I was no longer a walking drugstore, I remained sick. I was not cured—I would never be cured—and I needed to devote my energy to getting better. I wanted to get a job to fill my time, but that was not what I needed. I needed to get healthy. I needed to eat well, maybe cook some healthy meals, to sleep well, to do yard work, to help out Dad with work around their house, to help my wife, to be a father. That's what my therapist was saying and she was right. And given all the stresses that Jill had been through and the countless logistical and emotional burdens my illness had placed on her, and given the miscarriage and then the birth of our son and Jill's taxing (if rewarding) job as a nurse and my job loss, her situational depression needed to be addressed.

We needed to make a change.

I convinced Jill that we should move. I felt as if my family was invading my space. As much as I loved them and they loved me, right then, in that frame of mind, I convinced myself that I could not get healthy in Buffalo. We could not get healthy there.

I needed out, I needed something different, and Arizona was the only answer I could come up with. And just like that, we decided to move. We held an estate sale. We sold our dream home.

Who said I could be impulsive?

I never considered that I would have to find a whole new set of doctors. More importantly, though, I was so wrapped up in our move that I did not notice just how out of it Jill was. Normally, she would have been the one to lead the job of packing up the house, with me helping out (or me helping out a lot, if I was hypomanic). But she did almost no packing. She was depressed and overwhelmed. I packed everything besides her personal things, like clothes and toiletries. At least my mother noticed: During the packing, she would ask me, "How's Jill doing?" because *she* could see perfectly well that Jill was struggling. Mom needed me to see that, too. I did not notice it the way I should have.

Overall, my family did not understand the move. I couldn't blame them. Why were we leaving *now*? And with a new baby?

Also: Had I not learned my lesson, after leaving the NFL and thinking that everything would be different, that change of location does not necessarily make a significant difference? Was being surrounded by sunshine and Ponderosa pines somehow going to cure me, finally, of my mental illness?

~

The decision to move to Arizona was not just about mental states (I told myself), but also about geography, weather, lifestyle.

But let's be honest: Mental state was always front and center—and not just mine anymore. Anticipation of the move, then the move and initial relocation, stressed me out. There was finding a place to live. Having no job. Jill needing to find a new job (though because she's truly amazing at what she does, I didn't think that would be tough). The baby. And on and on.

We rented a small townhouse outside of Phoenix, with a plan to buy a house once we got settled.

It seemed great, at first. I didn't even seek out new doctors right away.

But Jill's depression was evident. Everything she had been through over the past several years and more had come at a cost. It was the unknown of what her life, our life, would be, now that she knew her husband had a mental illness.

The stress of her situation triggered something in me.

I ran every day. My energy level climbed and climbed. Any residual depression in me began to subside. I felt amazing, though I was again on the path to self-destruction. I barely slept, averaging about four hours a night. My metabolism sped up. I followed a strict diet. I dropped 50 pounds in five months. I was still sick, though I thought I was on the correct medication (I was not). My emotions soared. Once, at sunrise, while jogging in the mountains, I stopped to take in the breathtaking view, the glow of city lights, the sun rising over the mountains. I felt a surge of euphoria, warmth, love. I began to cry. My endorphins, along with other brain chemicals, must have been flooding my system. It was like being on Ecstasy without taking the pill, a high that's indescribable. The upside of bipolar.

I was hypomanic for six months.

And of course things *weren't* amazing. They *weren't* perfect. In my hypomanic state, my incredible energy wasn't burned off simply by going off to run and commune with nature. I would turn all my attention and focus on whoever was near me that I knew—and since it was just Jill and me (and baby Connor), she continued to bear the brunt. I deeply regret it but I can't deny it: I spent a lot of energy telling Jill things she was doing wrong (being a less than perfect parent to Connor, not shopping for or cooking dinner), and giving her my opinion on who she was (not being forthcoming with me about the extent of her condition, even though I had done exactly that and more with her). In the state I was in, there were no positives. Almost nothing about what I said was true. Still, it hurt Jill terribly. In fact, it saddened her beyond belief. But I couldn't control myself. It was the illness talking, not me—but then, how could I separate one from

the other? How could she? How can any loved one of someone who's mentally ill? We could not agree on anything. We
fought about everything. I didn't notice just how small she
was feeling. She was seeing a therapist, and then we started
seeing someone together.

I finally found a new psychiatrist, something I should
have done right when we moved to Arizona. He made a
small adjustment to my medication which helped my mania
subside a bit. Then, in the spring, still wired and angry, I
went to see Lisa, a new therapist. She was helpful but my
symptoms did not magically disappear. I saw her on my own,
and then Jill and I saw her together, to further understand
how to live with and understand bipolar. We became very
close with our doctors: With no family and very few friends
around, they became our support system. It was just us and
now ten-month-old Connor, stuck in a small townhouse in
the middle of the desert. We had to figure it out on our own.

Week by week, session by session, Lisa showed that she
was someone who got me. She was young and we could talk
about anything. She understood and was familiar with sports,
and had lots of professional athletes as clients. She was cul-
tured and traveled a lot. Sometimes it took me a while to
understand her message to me. Sometimes I felt like she had
to keep explaining and explaining until I finally got it. It was
probably my fault, or maybe that's the way the hard-fought
truths always work, no matter how smart you are (or think
you are).

Once, she pointed out that my personality, even when I
wasn't acting "sick," *seemed* low maintenance but that I was
in fact very high maintenance. All the time.

She taught me that anger was a teachable moment. She
taught me to breathe. When we met, she always asked me,

before anything else, "What's going well?" Sometimes it made me mad, maybe because it implied that lots of things obviously *weren't* going well.

She said that my football-playing mentality would help me in dealing with my illness. That I was "coachable."

Over time, I got better at therapy. Maybe it was because I was working with better doctors or because I tolerated bad ones for less time. Or maybe it was just me being better at it. I actually thought that was a lot of it: I was genuinely getting better at following the steps needed for healing. I started to realize that some of those sessions where you walk in thinking you have things figured out, or there's nothing in particular to figure out that day, are the sneaky ones that actually lead to real progress because, well, you never know.

While I was hypomanic, I began a job search and was offered a position in construction sales. The offer prompted me to do some online research about the company and the position I was considering. Then I researched how to handle bipolar disorder in the workplace. I found some helpful, sane-sounding advice: Take regular breaks *before* you think you need them; try a relaxation exercise, such as deep breathing; take a walk around the block; listen to relaxing music; call a friend; take time off for counseling. Mostly, though, they advised you not to share your bipolar diagnosis with anyone in the workplace. If you must, share it with only a very few trusted co-workers.

I was disappointed to realize just how much I agreed with the advice.

During my most difficult times, I wanted to share details of my illness with whomever I wished, including work colleagues. Yet that was probably a bad idea. Mental illness has always been a fact to keep secret. And no matter how complex it is—and it is incredibly complex—it is too often treated as a simple "Does he or doesn't he?" question. You can't talk about it in all its nuances. Having mental illness is taboo. Being mentally ill is stigmatizing. For all the strides we've made, mental illness remains unaccepted and poorly understood. Why should the workplace be any different? At my medical device job, I had gone an entire hellish year keeping my illness a secret from everyone but my boss, and boss's boss, before I resigned. So when I read the "wisdom" of websites on the proper approach to disclosing or not disclosing your mental illness at work, it struck a nerve. I felt sympathy for all those who live with a mental illness and have to balance it with the demands of the workplace. I thought of the psychiatric nurse at the support group meetings.

I emailed a lawyer who often worked with former NFL players, and explained my situation. I didn't know if I could work, I wrote. He called me and asked a few simple questions. By the end of the call, he expressed confidence that the NFL would put me on disability.

How strange: It was just a few years before that I had had a job that was so public, the NFL, and experienced just about the most public glory anyone can have from their job, winning the Super Bowl. (Maybe only being an astronaut and landing on the Moon tops that.) Then I had a job where I had to remain silent about the most influential thing in my life. Then I was unemployed. Now, I had to figure out if I could work again and, if I could, how I would pull that off. Quite a fall from grace.

By the time I had finished reading those websites about keeping quiet at work regarding one's bipolar, I had decided on another huge life change.

~

Jill was seeing a psychiatrist. He put her on an antidepressant. After a few months, she was feeling better. It didn't change our situation, but it made it easier for her to handle the situation.

It hadn't been pure depression that was burdening Jill. It was many different things. She had started back on birth control after having Connor, and shortly after that her symptoms started. It didn't bother her mentally so much as it depleted her physically. Her mind felt good, she said, but her body was completely exhausted. Now *she* wanted to lie down and/or sleep at all times. She had no energy for anything. No energy to take care of herself, Connor, or me. She wasn't able to work as hard as she always had. She didn't even want to do the fun things. Yet no one knew the cause. It took months, and many doctors—a naturopathic doctor, an endocrinologist, then her ob-gyn, the one who actually made the correct diagnosis that it was the birth control, which had suppressed her estrogen level to that of a sixty-five-year-old post-menopausal woman. She stopped taking the birth control immediately but it still took months for her body chemistry to get right again. Add to this my occasionally hypomanic state, the unpleasant and occasionally cruel things I was often saying to her during it, the fact that we were all alone together in Arizona, and it was no wonder she was having so much trouble. And I couldn't even say "we were all alone together." In fact, when I was in a hypomanic state, as when I was in a severely depressed state, she didn't really *have* me, the Keith that she had fallen in love with, her best friend, her closest companion. She felt like she had lost me. That she was truly all alone.

She had always been a person who does the right thing. She had organized our life to make it perfect. But that plan wasn't working. And that result wasn't possible.

The first year in Arizona was extremely tough on our marriage. If we wanted yet another test—we did not—we had gotten it.

~

This is not the "spiritual awakening" part. Just the next part.

Sometime after my suicide attempt, my in-laws gave me a daily devotional to read, called *The One Year Uncommon Life Daily Challenge*, co-authored by my former coach, Tony Dungy. One challenge in particular hit me: Advice For High-Anxiety Moments: "'This is my command—be strong and courageous! Do not be afraid or discouraged. For the Lord your God is with you wherever you go'" (Joshua 1:9).

Maybe it struck me because the authors of the book had linked it with "high anxiety," which sounds like such a modern condition—but of course it's not. People have been feeling that as long as there have been people. For as long as there have been people, there have been people who have been afraid and discouraged, experiencing all sorts of "high anxiety" moments. How do we come out of them? *Can* we come out of them? The passage above references the time after Moses has died, and Joshua has been chosen by God to lead the Israelites into the Promised Land.

I did not see myself as Joshua and I was not leading anyone to the Promised Land. But the passage spoke to my desire for purpose and responsibility, to somehow find a way to "lead"—or at least connect with—those who were suffering from what I was suffering from. I appreciated the relevancy of the passage, how contemporary it sounded.

I could not keep hiding from others, or hiding from my responsibilities. Be strong! Be courageous!

Whatever the forces, I came to believe that things had unfolded as they had for a reason. I might not ever understand the reason, but it all helped to make me who I was. All the choices, misfortunes, triumphs, going to NAU, almost quitting, struggling to make the NFL, almost quitting, winning the Super Bowl, being bipolar, the great test on my marriage, even, ultimately, deciding to write my story: I had to believe there was some reason to how things happened. I did not believe in luck (yes, even though I'm Irish) and I was not one of those athletes so totally self-absorbed that I thought God had given me the strength to score a touchdown while somehow depriving my opponent from making *his* play to prevent the touchdown . . . so I'm not suggesting that the linebacker ahead of me on the depth chart breaking his leg was all about me. My destiny is not more important than anyone else's.

I just had to figure out how to use what was happening to me in the best possible way. For me, for my family, and maybe even for others I didn't know.

The devotional hit me hard for another reason: I feared every day for the future. I had no job, no income, a baby, an illness I had not yet figured out, and after years of saying my thoughts about suicide were just that, and being sure of my own limits, I had recently overdosed on pills. And I had not just done it as a one-time blip but because a part of me truly wanted to die.

Be strong. Be courageous.

And then, like that, I had had enough of hiding.

I logged onto my Facebook and made a new page. I included my bio, and revealed in it that I was bipolar.

I was diagnosed with bipolar disorder in 2010 . . .

Once I had written the whole thing, I did not hesitate to hit the "Share" button. Maybe it was a few years after the fact, but better late than *really* late.

Now everyone who knew me . . . knew. The oppressive secret I had kept was revealed. Knowing that felt liberating. I felt lighter. The rumors of my illness were confirmed. I no longer had to hide. I could move forward. People knew why I had disappeared.

I realized that the Facebook page wasn't for anyone but me. So I could breathe.

After posting my pronouncement where anyone could see it, I put Connor in the kid seat of our car and drove to Costco. It was there that I decided to turn down the construction sales job. I would devote as much of my time and effort as possible to raising mental health awareness.

Then I bought twenty rolls of paper towels. It felt great. I had a plan.

~

After I went public with my illness, it took time before I heard from some of the former teammates with whom I had been fairly close. I didn't hold it against them. I was pretty sure it took time because of how difficult a subject it is to bring up.

It's not fair to focus on the reaction, or nonreaction, of ex-teammates: It was most people. Childhood friends. College buddies. Neighbors. Even some family members. Few people reacted with a "What happened?" or a "How are you doing?" I was quite sure that had my Facebook post revealed that I had cancer, I would have been overwhelmed by cards and flowers. People would be baking cookies and running marathons for me.

"Mental illness is not a casserole illness," a friend who "got" it told me. "Don't expect people to stop by with food."

Not every reaction was like that. I was often pleasantly surprised by people. I ran into a friend of my sister's who none of us had seen for years. After a few pleasantries, much less than you would expect for an absence that long, she asked, "How are you doing? How's your mental health? I read your blogs on Facebook." I was stunned—and moved. A person who actually knew how to talk to someone with mental illness!

There were others like that.

Almost exactly the same time that I resolved to turn down the construction sales job, the NFL contacted me. I had been granted Total and Permanent Disability Benefits. Because I was a veteran of more than four years—those extra two weeks that my agent Jack had negotiated with the Colts over how long it takes to heal from a busted rib—I would get very decent coverage.

And with that, I decided to write my story. I decided to start a foundation to raise awareness about mental illness and raise money for research and other support. I wrote up plans. My enthusiasm could take me a long way, at least to start. I was stoked.

I strolled into my therapist's office without a care in the world—or so I thought. I had just had a very productive four-hour phone call with Jimmy, my long-time friend and confidant who was helping me to start my foundation. We had just solved all kinds of logistical issues and, while we were at it, a few of the world's problems, too, I thought. I felt great when I walked through the door and took my seat on Lisa's couch.

"Keith, let's check in," she said. "How do you feel?"

"I'm so happy, so excited," I told her. "Things are going great. Let me tell you everything." I took a deep breath, unconsciously.

"How do you feel right now?"

"Great." *Had I not just told her that?* "I have great news. Not only about the foundation and my book, but with other things in my life. Let me tell you."

"You seem wound tight, a little frantic. How do you feel? How does your body feel?"

"Oh," I said, not expecting her assessment.

"Relax, Keith. Breathe." She waited a moment for me to follow her words. "How do you feel? Pay attention. How does your body feel?"

"My body is tired, so tired. Everything is heavy, my arms hurt. My heart is racing. I'm very anxious. But I am so happy. Everything is going great. I don't feel good. I'm shaky. I'm scared."

"You're in a hypomanic state," she said.

"No, I'm not," I said. "I am?"

"They don't all look and feel exactly alike," she said, again pausing for me to take stock. "Pay attention to your body and your breathing. Do you feel everything?"

I grew emotional. "Yes, I do. I feel like this often. Why do I feel like this? Is this a different kind of hypomania? Is this what it feels like? Why do I feel this way?"

"You're 'tired but wired.' It's okay. Embrace it. You can control it. Relax. Breathe. You can figure it out. You can use it for good. Embrace it."

After a moment following her words, I said, "Wow, I feel it all."

"Breathe," she guided.

~

There were, as she had said, different types of hypomania. In one instance, I might listen with the car radio blasting and be brought to tears. (I didn't do that very much anymore.) It was helpful for me to realize that different aspects of bipolar can manifest themselves in different ways and at different pitches, whether under medication or not. And it was important, as Lisa had said, to be aware of what precisely was going on, to take stock, to breathe, even to embrace it.

The troubling, or maybe more intellectual, part of that awareness, though, meant that so many different expressions of my personality could be pinned as bipolar. If I was consistently energetic? Bipolar. If I was up just a little? Bipolar. If I was down, either a little or a lot? Bipolar.

Happy? Bipolar. Sad? Bipolar.

Did that mean that *no* emotion was an expression of me, the real me? Was I just all one big bipolar reaction machine? Was there any Keith O'Neil apart from bipolar? Or were there many? I came across a quotation from a rapper named Zeco XQ, who wrote, "Bipolar is like having five different souls that fight for one body!"

~

I called my old college friend, C.R., who now lived in Cave Creek, Arizona, to find out the best tattoo artist in the

Phoenix area. "Tattoo Dave," C.R. said without hesitation. I called Tattoo Dave for an appointment. He must truly have been incredible because his first availability was half a year out. Hypomanic as I still was, I told him I didn't have six months. I begged him to get me in earlier.

He worked out of his house and told me to stop by to show him what I wanted. When I got there, he was in the middle of an inking session with someone. Dave himself was covered in tattoos, including his face and head. I'm sure that out in public, people judged him all the time, usually not with admiration.

I had Connor with me, in a stroller. I guessed that it was rare for a client to show up with a baby in a stroller.

As I explained to him what I wanted on my "half-sleeve," I was acting extremely impatient and agitated, though I couldn't help myself.

"What's your deal, man?" he asked me, straight up.

I didn't feel like hiding, even with someone I had met just five minutes before. "I'm bipolar and right now I'm hypomanic," I said without an instant's hesitation.

He could not have been cooler. "Okay," he said, with great sympathy. "I'll get you in in two weeks. In the meantime, just take care of yourself, okay?"

With Jill working closer to full-time hours as a nurse and with me on permanent disability, I became Connor's number one caregiver. I also became obsessed with running and hiking. Connor and running, hiking and Connor—those were the passions that kept me sane for a time. At least once a week, I would drive the thirty minutes out to the Superstition Mountains (the Sups), sometimes alone but mostly with Connor. If it was the both of us, I'd strap him on in a kiddie-hiking backpack and we'd head into the Sups, or we'd go to Sedona or sometimes the Grand Canyon. I climbed and reflected. The harder the climb, the better. The Arizona desert had a way of bringing me an incredible sense of peace—maybe it does that to everyone but I felt it powerfully, as if time had forgotten about this place. Maybe it was all the dead saguaro cacti lying burnt in the Arizona sun or my perception of the American Old West, which had barely changed since I was a child. Whatever it was, my worries vanished out there, and the deluge of thoughts that so often raced through my mind came to a halt. I could breathe. It's where I felt most alive.

I sat at a picnic table, gazing out at the mysterious Superstition Mountains. The Arizona sun was warm on my back, the air cool. Connor was on the ground, occupied by the countless grasshoppers hopping around him.

How did I get here?

Life got me here. My life got me to this picnic table. That was enough of an answer for me at the moment.

I wanted to put aside the *hows* of my life and the *whys*. Right then, I just wanted to watch my son play with grasshoppers.

As alluring and calming as it was for me out in the mountains, the incredible beauty of nature and the big sky and the room to roam, the idea that we would put down roots in Arizona and use it as our "starting over" place faded. As I got healthier, and Jill did, too, reality set in. We were all alone out here in Phoenix. Our occasional trips back East made us realize how much we had sacrificed.

My bouts of mania seemed to stop, though I didn't believe it was connected to my Facebook announcement. Then again, going public made it easier on my family, or so I thought.

I wanted to go home. Jill and I were ready to welcome the extra help. And now we both felt we were strong and healthy enough to make the move and start over . . . again.

And maybe the improvement in my condition was, if not totally connected to my going public, then at least not totally unconnected. Because now that I had done that, I could go further, share it with others, which gave me that motivation, which was sometimes tangled up with hypomania and even confused with it. It gave me a sense of purpose.

Arizona would always have a place in my heart not only because I went to college there, and met Jill there, but it was also where I found, eventually, a sense of equilibrium. It was where I found peace. During our two years there, my frequent explorations of the Grand Canyon, Sedona, the Sups, and more were the perfect opportunities to reflect, calm down, be lifted up. It was therapy without drugs and without talking. Maybe *where* is a more important question to answer than *how* or *why*.

~

Before I left Arizona, in early 2015, I went for my appointment with Tattoo Dave. My hypomania had subsided quite a bit since I had last seen him. We hit it off immediately. He was outspoken and forthright. We talked about everything: my illness, football, politics, everything. He had a reptile collection he was proud to show me. He was passionate about what he did and talented at it. He was passionate about life. You could tell he had a big, generous heart.

He shaded in clouds around the Celtic cross I had on my arm and added tats in an angel on the back of my arm. Next, he tattooed a Bible and a cross on my chest, a "chest plate."

This guy with tattoos covering his face and head made me feel so normal by the way he treated me and how open he was to talk about bipolar and mental illness. He was so matter of fact about it. I thought, *How great would it be if all society could look at it the way Tattoo Dave does, with no stigma attached?* With him, I did not feel the need to change subjects if I didn't want to. He accepted me, illness and intensity and all. That's who I was. It made me me.

He was so moved by our session that he asked me if, before I headed East, I would visit a friend of his who was struggling with many of the things I had been dealing with. I was honored to. It furthered that sense of purpose I wanted to feel.

The whole encounter was helpful. I thought back to it later, when I overheard someone say, "Who needs a therapist when you have a tattoo artist?"

Chapter 12

FROM CHAOS COMES CLARITY

There are patterns in your life, whether you notice them or not.

Following my diagnosis of bipolar disorder, I found myself facing a goal similar to trying to make an NFL roster. There, I had wanted something bad enough to work incredibly hard for it.

It was the same thing all over again, only this time I wanted to be well. And finding wellness was a bigger challenge than making an NFL team. Playing professional football was a job, one that would end, and sooner than later. Finding wellness could last a lifetime, or at least I hoped it would.

It became my number one goal.

And though finding wellness was going to be greater than the pursuit of NFL success, the football challenge gave me hope for the wellness one. After all, during my four-plus-year career, I was always a "bubble player," someone who had to fight each season to make the roster, unsure whether my pursuit was a success until the final preseason game, hoping as the days wound down that this wasn't the one that dead-ended with a visit from The Turk. My salary was always the league minimum. I was mainly a special teamer, a position usually taken for granted (no matter how much it mattered to Coach Parcells).

My success at football was the result of several things: Giving full effort on every play. Knowing my strengths and weaknesses. Immersing myself in what I needed to know to get better—studying the playbook, watching film, weight-lifting even though I hated weightlifting, etc.

Now, in my new pursuit, I had to do the same thing: Be very deliberate and figure out what it was I needed to do to be successful.

One of my main fights: I could be self-absorbed. I didn't mean to be. I liked to be around people. I cared about others. But often I was way too much in my own head, which could come off as selfish, even though I knew I wasn't.

Second, related to the first: I had to fight my resistance to keep out family, which I did (except for Jill), and friends, which I did (except for Phil). They wanted to help me but didn't know how. Because I didn't know how to help myself, I had to understand how to do that, and make it easier on them—not resent them or distance them because they couldn't.

I had come up with a way to combine these goals, which were both about looking outward. If my number one purpose was to find wellness, I could make it a less lonely journey if I actively included others in it. My new purpose was not just to get well but to find wellness while sharing my story. Selfishly, I knew that this less self-oriented approach had the ability to speed up my own search for wellness. How did I know that? Because I had spent years in the depths of depression and mental illness, fighting every day for purpose. During that period, I could not happily work, exercise, or communicate with others. I would go through days without leaving my bed or even eating. My idleness, my isolation, my lack of engagement with the world caused me to slowly go insane. My suicide attempt was an acknowledgment that I had given up hope that any purpose was out there. Or a purpose for me, at least.

Enough about me. I would find purpose through people I didn't know—though I actually *did* know them. With each blog entry I wrote and posted, I felt as if I was sending, through my laptop screen, an SOS, extending a hand to others just like me that I knew were out there.

My purpose was to spread the message to never give up. The message of the importance of paying attention to mental health and working toward better understanding, treatment, maybe even cures. I had already started an organization that funded related research. I would find purpose through mental illness, the very thing that tried to kill me.

For my whole life, I had tried to run from it, had tried to quit it, and I had failed. Now I was going to embrace it.

Breathe.

~

I sought opportunities to speak at local high schools and organizations. I knew that the "Super Bowl champion" part of my biography would help get me in the door. I would always wear the huge ring. I'm sorry, but when the light catches that many diamonds, people notice.

To get through the talks, though, I needed help. To sleep the night before a presentation, I often had to take an Ambien. Minutes before I went on stage, I would usually take Klonopin (anti-anxiety) and Propranolol (lowers the heart rate). Radio interviews were a little easier because you don't have an auditorium or gym full of people out there looking at you, eagerly awaiting your next word.

And no, public speaking did not get better with "practice," at least not for me. Each occasion had the potential to be as terrifying as the one before.

But it was working. The more I spoke, the more people approached to tell me their story, or wrote to me on my Facebook or visited the website I had created and left comments there.

I just read your story about "recovery" & bipolar disorder. I don't know if you have time to read all your messages, but what you described is so like my life. I was diagnosed with bipolar in 2002, got proper medication in 2005 & continue to see a psychiatrist in 2014. Please know how much you talking about your experiences means to me. Every year I'm a bit better . . . longer periods of feeling good . . .

WOW!!!! You have my symptoms pegged!! I have suffered all my life with a disabling depression roller coaster, and also temporary paranoia. After the suicide of my beloved older brother due to bipolar, my life spun out of control like never before, and it has been a ten year fight to learn as much information and therapy as I could. Yet here I am, thank GOD!!!!

I am a 35 year old husband and father of two. I have struggled with bipolar for over 8 years. As a result of my struggles I was fired from a good job, about a year ago, and had to relocate my family to a new state, 12hrs from our home. I struggle with many things including my marriage, finances, and just getting up in the morning. I finally decided to do some digging to help me learn to manage and own my life. I found your 2014 post and it compelled me to write this. I am a sports fan and have a lot of respect for professional athletes. It takes a lot of focus and dedication to do what you do. Reading about an athlete that has found a way to live with this challenge is very promising. If you can reach your goals, then so can I.

Great stuff Keith. When I was playing basketball in college I found that practice and games were always the time I seemed to be able to control what was happening in my head the most. I too recently found out I have bipolar, something about sports seems to calm the mind and help achieve a sense of peace, at least for me personally

I don't include these messages to show what a great guy I was becoming, but to show how wide and deep the problem is. And for how many years those with diagnosed bipolar have suffered, and how silent they've stayed and felt they had to stay.

And those are just the ones who are self-aware enough, and cared for enough, to have been diagnosed. What about the others? Or the ones without health insurance coverage? Who's to say that group isn't even larger?

The stories always sounded familiar to me because there were so many elements similar to my own story. Sometimes addiction was included. They didn't always mention a suicide attempt or attempts—but they didn't have to. Often it wasn't the individual himself or herself who would approach me after my talk but a family member, often a parent, who wanted to tell me about the hell their child was going through in dealing with bipolar.

At one high school presentation, after I finished speaking, a young boy, maybe fourteen or fifteen years old, stood up and told the auditorium he had bipolar. He said it was the first time he had told anyone. There wasn't much more to it. I asked his first name, and thanked him for sharing, and then the presentation and the Q&A were over, and he picked up his backpack, slung it over his shoulder, and disappeared through the door.

Chapter 13

THE PRESENT (2015–2017)

It's another house. Smaller, but very nice. There's more than enough room in the yard for both boys eventually to run around and play hide-and-seek and manhunt and have their friends over to play bigger boy games. So far it's been up to me to make the major fixes to the place: Put in a deck, landscape, seed the grass, finish the basement, etc.

We're in Pendleton, New York, a different Buffalo suburb from the one we were in last time.

In January 2015, we left Arizona, the gorgeous scenery and endless sunshine. If you choose to move from Arizona to Buffalo, people look at you funny. If you do it in the dead of winter, you don't even bother trying to explain.

If I had wanted to see, yet again, how an overload of stresses might affect my mental health—another cross-country move, the punishing Buffalo winter, finding and acclimating to new doctors, Jill securing a new job—I had set up a perfect lab experiment. Even the return home, while something we were looking forward to, came with ambivalence. After all, the last time I had lived here, those last several months before we fled Buffalo, were the sickest, most unstable of my life, which is saying something. Was this move of ours a fresh start, or a return to something we would never want to repeat?

You know what, though? We were now around family—my parents, my siblings (Colleen, Drew, and their kids are in Cleveland, which isn't that far), my nieces and nephews. Connor now had cousins nearby. Soon enough, with the birth of Tanner, he had a brother.

I officially started my foundation, called 4th and Forever, devoted to raising awareness about mental illness. (The foundation name is a play on a football term.) My hope was that the foundation would also raise money to fund research. One area of particular interest to me: For those already suffering with mental illness, how can we minimize the added, prolonged pain and indignity of being a medication guinea pig? Is there any way to shorten or streamline that process? I did not assume it was easy to do or it would have been done already.

Helping me on the foundation were two businessmen with an affinity for startups, and a prominent mental health advocate who himself has bipolar, as well as deep philanthropic ties in western New York.

Two months after we returned east, I found a new therapist. Early in our first session, she asked me to gauge how

I thought I was doing, from 1 to 10. It happened that that day I felt like an 8, though that was very rare unless I was hypomanic. I told her I never expect a 10. I would aspire to making 8 my goal.

The therapist agreed that that was a good goal. She said that most people, including those without bipolar, would be thrilled to have an 8 every day, or even just most days. Even just *some* days.

Jill found a job almost immediately, this time at a pediatric and adolescent urgent care facility. Her hours are 4 p.m. to 11 p.m., three days a week. She often doesn't get home until past midnight.

On days when Jill works, I am the primary caretaker for the boys. I wake up when they do, between 6:30 and 7:30. I feed them. Connor is the pickiest eater on Earth. Getting him to eat yellow food is no problem—cereal, waffles, orange juice. We have to work on the other colors. Tanner is still on baby food.

I either take Connor to school or, if it's not a school day, he'll watch TV or do other activities until about 10, when I put Tanner down for a nap. I typically nap on the couch while Tanner sleeps and Connor watches TV. Or he'll play on my phone, often YouTube clips of kids playing or Legos. We also play Candyland and Chutes and Ladders. Or we'll read books—his favorites are *Goodnight, Goodnight, Construction Site* and *The Alphabet Construction Book*. Maybe he'll be the one in the family who goes into construction.

When Tanner gets up, I feed him and Connor lunch. I don't have any specialties yet but I can cook if I'm in the mood. Then we do something active outside. I'll put Tanner in the stroller and we'll walk around the neighborhood while Connor rides his bike with training wheels. We go to the park that has the huge jungle gym. I play T-ball and soccer with him. Tanner will sit and watch, eyes wide with interest, usually with a smile.

Connor is laughing all the time. My parents have ten grandchildren and say that he's the happiest of them all. That makes me feel good. He loves spending time with his grandparents and cousins. He loves to wrestle. As much as we're together, he adores his momma.

Tanner is the happiest little baby. He smiles at anything. He's so easy—he rarely cries and he sleeps like an angel. He's just now developing a personality of his own.

If Jill is working that particular evening, I typically take the boys to my parents' house for dinner. My parents are a big help with them. If I don't get over there, I go a little nuts alone at our house all day with the kids.

If Jill's not working that day, we make dinner together, or now and then we'll go out with the kids. That's not too common since it's hard to get around with the baby. Our favorite place is reliable old Olive Garden, though we do a lot of carry-out from Wegmans, our local grocery store.

Then it's time to put the kids to bed around 7:30. Bath, bottle, books, story time, I can do it all. That's a typical day. I usually get in bed around 10 p.m. I tend to fall asleep quickly and stay asleep until the kids wake. I don't really have a ritual before bed. I might watch TV or listen to music on my headphones, mostly reggae or especially 311, the band I have listened to most consistently since I was a teenager to now, and whose music has sort of been the soundtrack of my life.

I know: solid, regular nights of sleep. How amazing is that?

I think about it the moment I wake up. I can't *not* think about it because I have to take my medication, twice a day, morning and night. It's usually nine pills in the morning and four at night. The number varies with my situation. If I'm feeling more anxious or having a hard time sleeping, I'll take the pills that help me with that. If I forget to take any meds, I just take them the following day and don't feel the effects because most of the drugs are already built up in my system.

The medication adjustment is a never-ending cycle. I just recently switched to a new drug. The one it replaced was making me feel more down and unstable. Among other medication, I currently take lithium, a mood stabilizer. I recently started taking Depakote (another mood stabilizer) again, and Abilify, an anti-psychotic. I also take Klonopin, as needed, for anxiety, and Ambien, also as needed, for sleep. I'm finally off of all the antidepressants. There's still debate over whether antidepressants can treat bipolar disorder effectively. From my personal experience, they don't—for me, anyway. Antidepressants plunged me into mixed states, which hugely, negatively affected my ability to be well. I haven't had a truly—*truly*—manic phase for over a year.

For now I'd call my mood stable, but I wonder how much is due to my lifestyle, the rhythm of my days, and my parental obligations. It's got to be some of that, though it definitely can't be all.

Medication alone does not bring health and peace to those who live with bipolar. It is just one piece of the puzzle. For me, being physically active is very important. Running long distances brings me clarity, sanity. I know how to breathe better. I'm better equipped to use the tools I've been given. I feel greater empathy with my fellow human beings, particularly those suffering with mental illness. I know I'm better today than I was yesterday. The greatest tool, I've learned, is time.

Continual support from family and friends is crucial. For me, faith in a higher purpose is also very, very important. You can define that purpose however it works for you. I have yet to speak with someone struggling to handle bipolar disorder who doesn't have faith in *some* type of higher power.

All of these matter. I know I have an immediate purpose—raising my boys—and a longer-term one—raising awareness about mental illness, and going out and talking about what I have and will always have.

But though I know all this, the willingness to follow and do and believe in what makes me feel better still fluctuates pretty widely, based on my mood. I do not have an official job. I work on my foundation, which is starting to grow. I recently gave speeches to both the Brain and Behavioral Research Foundation and the International Bipolar Foundation, two excellent organizations. Although things are better now than they were the last time I was in Buffalo, and better than they were for a good part of Arizona, I sometimes feel as though I just exist. And even the "higher purpose" that I have and pursue can start to elude me.

Sometimes I have to fight just to make it through the day. Today, for example, right this hour and the few hours before that and probably the rest of the hours until I go to bed, has been a hard one. There are lots of days when I don't want to get out of bed, but I know I can't do that since I'm a father. (My therapist calls bed my "cocoon," because that's the only place I feel completely safe and comfortable.) It's more lack of motivation than depression. It's nothing at all like the depression I went through. But I can have a hard time looking forward to days as a stay-at-home dad. One of my friends sells insurance and travels all the time and says he would do anything to quit his job and be a stay-at-home dad. Maybe my occasional difficulty is an ingrained sense of "man purpose" that "work" means leaving the house and going someplace outside the home for your job.

I'm thankful that I'm healthier than before, and more knowledgeable. Knowledge is power. When I think back to the undiagnosed me, I see not only a very anxious, troubled person but a very confused one. I had no idea what was going on. That makes the terrible feeling so much worse, like you're in a dark room, only you can't feel the floor or the walls and you're not sure if there's a ceiling or any way out. Now, at least, I understand why I am the way I am. That brings me peace.

At the same time, the label of being bipolar—*having* bipolar—and knowing I always will be can bring me down. It's not all gone. It never will be.

You can understand that you are the way you are without knowing *who*, really, you are. That's one thing that makes living with bipolar disorder tricky. Too often I ask myself, *Who am I? Who is the actual me? What's the inner me? What's my soul like? Am I the life of the party I was tonight or the recluse I was yesterday? Am I a happy person or a grouch, a bear? Am I controlled by my anxieties or am I filled with euphoria? Am I irritable or am I caring? Who's in control here?* Maybe I'm hanging out in the garage of a friend, and we're just bullshitting, and I'm drinking a beer (I will have a drink now and then; I don't get drunk) and having fun, and I stop myself for a moment to think . . . *Wait, is this me, finally?* I'll be in the car, listening to music real loud, and singing real loud . . . Is that me? I'll go over to my parents' house and just flop down on their couch, a little bearish . . . Is that me?

Which state is actually me?

"Okay, is *this* the real me?" I'll ask Jill sometimes, after I've been consistently happy for a few days.

Because I don't know the answer to that one. I don't think anyone does for him or herself, not even those free of mental illness. We're all born with a little something wrong.

Yet I wonder how my different moods affect those who love me. I realize how tough it has been and continues to be on them. Do they still feel that they have to walk on eggshells around me? Do they have to "prepare" for me? I recently talked with my parents about this. They said they always try to figure me out as soon as I walk in the door. Do I immediately go to the couch and flop down? Do I walk around a lot, pacing? Do I announce that I just mowed the yard, worked out, went to the store, etc.? They can tell pretty quickly what condition I'm in. But it doesn't change how they treat me. "We don't know which Keith is coming over but it doesn't matter," says my dad. I've lived with a mood disorder my whole life, one that wasn't diagnosed until a few years ago, so why should the label change anything? I'm the same me they've always known.

Then again, everyone is different. For me, some days are much more difficult than others—but how is that different from other people? Maybe it is at the edges, the extremes. No, they don't have to fight to beat their disease. But they still have to fight, day by day.

Like I said, today is a tough one. I got up, went for a 3½-mile walk and came home and still felt like shit. So I slept for another three hours, off and on.

Over the past few years I've learned to be more self-aware, more conscious of my moods. I understand them and welcome them. I don't do much to try to alter them. Just take my meds, try to exercise, and remain content with who I am.

~

Of course, I worry that one of my sons is going to have bipolar. It's genetic. I don't want either of them to have to live with this.

I can't let this disorder get the best of me as a father. For example, if I feel depressed, I can't deal with it just by lying on the couch all day. I can't let the boys see me that way. I can't be The Bear. I have to try extremely hard to not let my moods control me. For their sake, not mine.

As far as raising them the right way: I don't think that will be a problem. Plus, I've got Jill. They have Jill. We all have Jill.

~

I can't lie: Being hypomanic is great. I get things done! I run a lot, I clean the house, I write, I run errands, I run again. I wake up very early with energy from the get-go. Music sounds almost indescribable: It's not as if I'm "just" listening to it. It's coming from inside my body, as if my body is the vehicle for the sound. I love it. Unfortunately, all the things that I do that feel great feed the hypomania, which makes me even more hypomanic. It's like I said earlier about some drugs: The more you do, the more you want. And, like drugs, hypomania can be dangerous. If I don't control it, I could eventually go into full mania.

My mom says she loves when I'm in this hypomanic state. I'm engaging, fun to be around, helpful. I set the table unasked, do the dishes, etc. I don't just lie on the couch like I often do. "When you're hypomanic, you're Keith," my Mom told me recently.

"No, I'm always Keith," I remind her, "whether I'm up, down, or anything in between."

Jill is also fine with the hypomanic me. She keeps a close eye on me but lets me do my thing. If I want to get up at 4 a.m. to unload the dishwasher, fine. If I want to run around the neighborhood at the crack of dawn, fine. She doesn't say much and, like my mom, she kind of enjoys it. Her only concern is that I don't get *too* high.

But there are negatives to my hypomania aside from its being a gateway to full mania—my mind racing, my pacing, my inability to sleep without the help of medication, my shorter attention span. With the good comes the bad. Fortunately, I've learned to recognize the red flags. Two years ago, five years ago, I couldn't recognize these symptoms and, as a result, I would climb the mountain of mania. Today, I take steps to make sure I don't spiral out of control. I take my medication, I try to relax, I see my therapist, I limit the hypomanic "feeders." I breathe. It's a great feeling to know I have my illness *somewhat* figured out. It's something I've worked at very hard.

I called my therapist yesterday after I recognized my hypomanic state and she said, "Pace yourself. Spend two hours a day working on the book, then close the laptop and you're done for the day. Finished. Don't feed the mania, don't feed the monster. Set aside time to rest and do things that are mindless, like watching college football. Don't forget to relax. And breathe."

It's nice having someone in my corner providing these tips.

So what do I do now—today, I mean? It's been almost exactly two hours. I've been writing while listening to music.

I am going to remove the headphones.

I am going to shut down my computer for the rest of the day.

And I'm going to sit on my couch and watch a football game featuring my alma mater, Northern Arizona University. Let's see them kick some ass!

⁓

There is no cure for bipolar disorder, but there are ways to live a happy, healthy life with it. Like my goal of playing in the NFL, you must be willing to put in time and dedication. It will be more difficult for some than others. It took me about three years from when I was diagnosed until I found consistent wellness, and I still have to work at it daily.

If you're battling bipolar disorder or another mental illness, here are some tips that helped me. I hope they help you, too. At this stage in my story I don't think I have to point this out, but I will anyway: I am not a doctor or therapist. What follows are simply "rules" that have helped me.

- Find a higher power or purpose. It takes many forms. Find the one that works for you.
- Find a doctor you can relate to. Some doctors work better with some patients than others. Choose wisely and always get a second opinion.
- Find a therapist and talk their ear off. It's nice to talk with someone who understands and is familiar with your illness.
- Take your medications and know them well. Understand how your medications interact with other medications; know how your medications interact with you and your illness. Medication is key to recovery so it's important that you, not just the person prescribing it, know how it feels and works.

- Don't be afraid to share with someone that you have a mental illness. Chances are considerable that they either have one also or know people who do. This will allow you to vent. It's nice to get it out. Holding it all in makes things worse—for me, anyway. It caused anguish for way longer than I probably would have experienced it.
- Study your illness. In the long run, at some point, your knowledge and understanding will pay off.
- Get out of the house. Call friends and family, visit with them, and try your best to stay social even if it's the last thing you want to do.
- Exercise. Easier said than done, I know. Even a walk will do.
- Eat three meals a day and drink plenty of water. Stay healthy.
- Remain in the present. Try to not worry about the past or the future.

My résumé is shot. I haven't worked in almost five years. And if a potential employer asked me why I haven't worked in five years and I gave an honest answer, I am almost certain I wouldn't get the job.

The future is my biggest fear, especially if I lose my disability from the NFL. I don't know if I could handle that. I don't know what I would or could do for a living. My biggest fear is providing for my family. And since stress triggers episodes and anxiety . . . it's a bad cycle to contemplate.

But I have surrounded myself with great doctors and therapists. My psychiatrist now gives me 30 minutes whenever I feel the need. My wife and family understand me and my illness way more than before. If everything could stay the way it is right now, I think I would continue to improve.

Jill and I are in a much better place with each other. Since moving back east, we've gone to marriage counseling just twice, and we didn't argue or fight during the sessions. We were understanding with each other, patient, loving. Nothing like it was in Arizona, where we bit each other's head off at almost every session. Things have improved. Like most marriages, ours is evolving and maturing. But I think we're ahead of the game (not that I'm turning it into a competition with others) because we had to endure so much at the beginning of our marriage. Now, we feel as if we can take on just about anything.

On the anniversary of my diagnosis or the anniversary of my suicide attempt, we talk about it and reflect on how far we've come in a relatively short time. Those days are always strange, though. I don't know why Jill had that miscarriage and why it triggered me into hell. I don't know why I was born with bipolar. Maybe time will tell.

Remember the old friend and drinking buddy who said to me, after my football career ended, "Your life's over. The best part of your life is over. You're nothing now"? We buried the hatchet. He's doing well now. We're friends again.

That doesn't mean everything's all better. This past May, after a wedding in Michigan for my mom's side of the family, Kevin and I drove the five hours back to Buffalo, just the two of us, the first time in years we'd been alone together for that length of time. I was going on about trying to get a job, wanting a job, but feeling unsure that I could hold it; I was fidgety; I would lose concentration; I was anxious; I would fall asleep for stretches . . . I got the sense that it was the first time it truly hit Kevin how sick I was. He didn't say anything afterward. But if the roles had been reversed, I know it would have torn me up to see Kevin like that.

~

When I first heard the word "recovery" associated with mental illness I was surprised. I associate "recovery" with physical injuries. In football, recovery is measured in weeks or months, not years. Jack and the Colts wrestled over whether a broken rib typically takes two weeks or four weeks to heal, but they were at least in the same ballpark. Weeks, not years. Weeks, not a lifetime.

This time around, it's not my rib or MCL or shoulder that has to recover, but my mind. It has taken me years so far. Even though I will live with this illness for the rest of my life, in a sense I have recovered. I have healed. It doesn't mean it's permanent—hey, a broken rib can heal and then you can break it again—but my recovery is real. I have found it.

How can I trust myself that I have things "in check" when I once thought having suicidal thoughts was not the same as contemplating suicide or actually attempting suicide, and I turned out to be so horribly wrong? Because things are not so brand new to me now. At this point, I have experienced so many highs, lows, and in-betweens. So, actually, I kind of *do* know when I have things "in check." It took years of learning about my illness and how to respond to my disorder. I am still learning, but I am not the same person I was five years ago.

Over the years I have done almost everything someone can do to recover from a major bipolar episode. I have willingly taken dozens of different medications to help stabilize my moods. I have spent hundreds of hours in talk therapy to help me understand how to live with this illness. I have been very vocal about my illness to help others and myself heal.

Sitting here, I realize the one thing that has helped in my recovery the most: time. Time really does heal. Time passes; I heal. Time has kindly given me my life back.

~

What defines me, as much as anything—way more than the Super Bowl ring on my finger—is my disease.

I don't have it. I *am* it.

More than a half-decade ago, I was disturbed by the thought that being bipolar would and could define me. How was that possible? How could I change that fact?

Today, after a long journey punctured by bizarre actions and scary thoughts, behavior I once wished I could take back only to realize that the behavior was a result of my disorder, and the disorder would accompany me for the rest of my life . . . I realized: no. As much as my therapist comforted me when she said I was not bipolar but only *had* bipolar, I realize how untrue that is. The softening of the description does not fit who I am.

I *am* bipolar.

My disorder *does* define me. It's who I am. It's how I think. It's my moods. It's why I experienced psychosis and lost touch with reality. It's why I was able to make the NFL as an undersized linebacker, which ultimately enabled me to win the ring I won. It's why I have such a great network of friends and family who have supported me before and after my diagnosis. It's why I have become so sensitive to others who struggle, because I now truly understand pain. It's why I challenged myself to speak less about my issues and me, and more words of encouragement for those similarly struggling. It's why I sleep a lot or not at all, sometimes for days. It's why I become hypomanic and incredibly creative during those periods. It's why my wife loves me and my sons adore me.

Some of my closest friends have recently opened up to me about their emotional and/or mental problems—but they won't go see a therapist. They see it as a sign of weakness or indulgence. Or they feel they just "don't know how to do it," or what they would say, week after week. They don't want the stigma.

Some more comments I have received from strangers:

Thank you Keith for being a voice for so many who deal daily, and often silently, with bipolar disorder. I couldn't agree with you more about the need to have support from friends and family. For so long . . . I believed I was alone in all of this . . . that's what this disorder can make a person believe!

Just wanted to thank you for what you are doing. Bipolar I has recently affected our family and has been a nightmare. You are an inspiration. Keep up the great work. Thank you again.

hi keith i was directed here by my favorite band korn i heard about your story on the news i think its badass your tackling mental illness more people need to be aware of mental diseases myself i suffer from a very hardcore case . . .

Thank you for helping those of us dealing with mental illness. My 10yr old struggles with bipolar disorder. It is nice to see support when some many people run or choose not to be involved in this issue.

Keith, Not only was I moved by your candor, I was inspired. It appears you've found your passion, and a passion that is truly special! It takes a big man to do what you've set out to do. and by doing so, you will make not only your mark, but in addition, helping others. Very cool, my friend. All the best wishes.

Maybe there *is* crying in football.

Looking back, it sometimes feels as if my life happened to someone else named Keith O'Neil. I won't ever forget how often I was dead certain that the nightmare would never end.

Now, I'm thankful it's all out in the open. Something good has come of it. A decade ago, you could have offered me all the money in the world to speak in public about this and I would have turned you down without a second's hesitation. Now I do it often, even if I still get nervous, sometimes terrified. My life now is to try and help bring peace to others like me— but who are not yet as far along. Earlier this year I attended a Buffalo Bills game. It was a rare occurrence because I almost never go to football games and rarely watch them on TV, not even the Super Bowl. As I was leaving, a middle-aged couple stopped me and asked if I was Keith O'Neil.

Yes, I said.

"We heard you speak last week at Corning," said the woman, starting to choke up. "You're touching so many lives."

More than seventy thousand people were spilling out of the stadium. I used to play in front of that many people, and millions more watching on TV. That could not compare to the satisfaction I got from seeing that woman's tears.

Bipolar magazine wrote a story on me. They were going to put me on the cover. When the magazine came out, I gave a bunch of copies to my mother who wanted to slip them into several offices in the university building where she worked. By the end of the week, both my parents called me, excitedly, to say that multiple people they knew had picked up the magazine, read the story, and actually wanted to talk with them, or me, about mental illness. They had a son or a daughter or a niece or a sibling or a partner who . . .

Because of course they did.

~

I'm sitting at a picnic table in a park not far from our home in Pendleton, our hometown. Connor is playing on the red-and-yellow jungle gym a few feet from me. I'm tapping away at my laptop keyboard.

I can't help but notice how in tune I am with my surroundings and myself. I am okay living in this exact moment. I can do it, maybe even better than people who are not mentally ill. I am completely content with life for the first time in many years. I could not care less about anything but watching my son play. I am enjoying time.

Jill is back at work. She is also doing a great job decorating the house. She is home right now with Tanner. I recently got TANNER tattooed over my heart, right below CONNOR.

We're planning the first fundraiser for my 4th and Forever Foundation. Mom's helping with the details. We raised enough money to give our first gift for bipolar research to the University at Buffalo. My friend and trusted advisor Jimmy is running in the New York City Marathon next fall to raise more funds.

I'm not sure if I will attend the tenth reunion of the Colts' Super Bowl victory, to be held this fall during halftime of one of their games. I don't want to be seen as "the sick one." *That* guy. Most of the fellows on the team didn't know what I was going through at the time. I guess I could attend the reunion and help some of them understand a little better—but then that would make it about me, and about bipolar. And it's a celebration of what we all did together, on the field.

Not long ago, my father confessed to me that he had always had his doubts that I would make it through college— not because he suspected mental illness but just because of how I was, how I handled things. Back then, he didn't think I would make an NFL team. Not that he didn't believe in me, but just because of the reality of the competition. As a football coach, he knew a few things.

Then he paused. He wanted to share something my mother's father once told him, comparing us as football players. "Your grandfather, my father-in-law, once said to me, 'Ed, you know more about the game than Keith. But Keith is a lot tougher than you.'"

As I sit here watching Connor, it's hard to believe I went through such difficult times, times when suicidal ideation invaded my thoughts and almost got the best of me. Times I sometimes wish I could forget. I know there are rough times ahead because this illness lurks and strikes when you're not paying attention. Yet even though it's not going away, not ever, I actually bask in this moment. Whatever is coming, it feels more like hills I'll need to climb, not mountains.

I look over at Connor, in his own world, then back at my laptop. I see the reflection in the screen. There's a smile across my face. I'm not just getting better, I *am* better.